MONEY 101

Money 101

MONEY 101

Your Easy Step-by-Step Guide to Enjoying a Secure Future

DEBRA WISHIK ENGLANDER

PRIMA PUBLISHING

PRIMA PUBLISHING and colophon are registered trademarks of Prima Communications, Inc.

Previously published under the title *How to Be Your Own Financial Planner* by Prima Publishing, 1996.

Library of Congress Cataloging-in-Publication Data

Englander, Debra Wishik.
     Money 101 : your easy step-by-step guide to enjoying a secure future / Debra Wishik Englander.
          p.   cm.
     Updated ed. of: How to be your own financial planner. Rocklin, CA Prima Publ., 1996.
     Includes index.
     ISBN 0-7615-0012-X
     1. Finance, Personal.   I. Wishik Englander, Debra. How to be your own financial planner. II. Title. III. Title: Money one hundred one
     HG179.W549 1997
     332.024—dc21   97-26576
                                                              CIP

97 98 99 00 01 AA 10 9 8 7 6 5 4 3 2 1

Printed in the United States of America

How to Order

Single copies may be ordered from Prima Publishing, P.O. Box 1260BK, Rocklin, CA 95677; telephone (916) 632-4400. Quantity discounts are also available. On your letterhead, include information concerning the intended use of the books and the number of books you wish to purchase.

Visit us online at http://www.primapublishing.com

CONTENTS

ACKNOWLEDGMENTS

I would like to thank the many planners, attorneys, and other financial experts whom I've interviewed for magazine and newspaper articles over the past decade. A special thanks goes to Stewart H. Welch III and his wife, Kathy. On short notice, both always answered questions on virtually every topic and managed to find me the perfect person to profile.

Thanks also goes to John Thornton for his persistence in pushing this project ahead and to Prima Publishing for believing in the book. Finally, thanks to my family, especially my daughter Elise, who tolerated the many hours I spent on the phone and working at the computer.

MONEY 101

INTRODUCTION

Unlike other professionals such as doctors and attorneys, anyone can say he or she is a financial planner. While the industry does recognize some designations, such as Certified Financial Planner and Chartered Financial Consultant, there is no direct government regulation of these positions. In fact, many accountants, lawyers, and insurance agents often serve as de facto financial planners for their clients.

Many people have turned to these "experts" out of necessity. If you are like most, your finances have gotten more complex along with other aspects of your life. Perhaps your full-time position is less secure so you have started a sideline business in order to pay your bills. You may be wrestling with the the issue of saving the ever-increasing amounts of money needed to send a child to college. Or you may have to figure out how to get first-rate medical care without going into debt. And, in terms of investing, the choices available for your assets are wider and

1

therefore also more daunting. For example, if you want to invest in mutual funds, you will have to choose from several thousand to select the funds that meet your needs. You may want to seek professional help at some point in your life as you address these complicated decisions, but you should never forget that *it is your hard-earned money.* After reviewing your options and doing some research, it is you who should make the final decisions on how to spend or invest your income.

By reading this book, you'll acquire a working knowledge of the basics of financial planning and will then be able to make more informed decisions about your money. If you feel capable of handling your own finances, you can immediately begin to take steps toward your future goals. And, if you do choose to use a professional planner, you will be a far more educated client and will be able to work that much better with your planner to make the most of your money.

WHAT IS FINANCIAL PLANNING?

To understand why people consult planners, you should first learn what is meant by the term "financial planning." Then, you can decide whether you're comfortable handling your own finances, or whether you want to consult a planner.

Financial planning is essentially the formation of a personalized plan that allows you to control your own financial destiny. This means you have a clear picture of your present financial situation: your net worth, your monthly obligations, your income, your savings, investments, and so on. Once you have this picture—which is what you and a planner would initially discuss—you can start thinking about a savings plan, an investment strategy, and whatever other financial goals you have.

The initial evaluation of your finances isn't necessarily complicated, except that most people either avoid thinking about their finances, or they worry about their money without taking any steps to alleviate these concerns. This trend may be changing, however. Last year, the top New Year's resolution among Americans was to improve their personal finances. For the first time, managing money was more important than losing weight or stopping smoking. You may think that you already have your finances under control. When you're up for a raise, you try very hard to persuade your employer that you need more than a 3 percent raise so that you'll beat inflation. You probably balance your checkbook with some regularity so that you don't bounce, say, your rent check. But these are just tiny slices of your financial pie. You have to start thinking about bigger issues, such as saving for your children's college education or your own retirement.

If you've just entered the workforce, you may shrug and wonder why you would have to manage your money. After all, your salary covers your rent and leaves you some spending money. That's true, but if you spend all your money, what will you do when you want to buy a new car or move to a more expensive apartment? Everyone, regardless of their income or amount of savings, should be paying attention to their finances.

Understanding your spending and savings habits isn't always pleasant. Perhaps you're a binge shopper, and while your checking account balance is shrinking, the contents of your closet are increasing. If you have a partner, maybe you don't even tell your spouse how much you're spending or how much you earn each week. The two of you must sit down together and work out a manageable budget. If you're having trouble working out a solution with your spouse, then you might want to sit down with a planner. The financial planner, as an objective third party, will ask both of you for details about your savings and your spending habits as well as your attitude toward money generally. A planner can serve as a conscience of sorts, as well as a referee if you and your mate have wildly different views about money. Likewise, a planner can assist during unanticipated financial crises such as a divorce, health problem, or death of a family member.

If you want your financial future—and your relationship—to be rosy, you will have to be honest about your money habits. Most likely, you and your significant other will have to adjust to each other's habits and make some compromises. Whether you talk between yourselves or consult a planner, you have to learn to carefully weigh financial issues and begin to make rational decisions, not just emotional ones.

You may feel comfortable making choices about your spending on your own, without seeking counsel from a planner. That's fine, but if you end up with more debt than you can handle or, on the other hand, if you're lucky enough to win the lottery, then you should speak with a planner. You may want to handle all your everyday financial decisions but consult an expert for one concern, such as estate planning or insurance issues. What's important is that you start monitoring your own finances so that you understand what you have, what you owe, and what financial goals you're working toward.

SPEAKING THE LANGUAGE OF FINANCIAL PLANNING

To evaluate all aspects of your financial situation, you need to review many items, including savings, tax planning, investments, insurance, and estate planning. Depending on your income, where you live, your family situation and other factors, some of these considerations can get complicated. However, it is possible for you to master the basics of all these issues. In fact, if you end up consulting a planner, it's critical that you understand why, for example, one type of investment is preferable to another or whether you need to buy more life insurance. If you're armed with this knowledge, you will be able to converse with a planner and easily understand his or her advice.

There's no doubt that the deregulation of the banking industry, tax reform, and the development of new investment vehicles contribute to your resistance to managing your money. And, with constant changes in stock prices, interest rates, and foreign economies, it may seem impossible to keep track of everything. However, by getting in the habit of reading a few consumer magazines, the financial section of the newspaper, and related books and products (some of which are free or available at minimal cost), you can get a relatively painless education about the basics of personal finance. With this information—the same a planner must absorb—you can begin to make sound decisions about your money.

HOW TO USE THIS BOOK

Depending on your financial expertise or interests, you may want to skim sections of this book while carefully reviewing other sections. However, if you are just starting out and haven't been paying attention to your finances, then you'll probably find the book most useful if you follow the chapters in order.

First, you will learn how to figure out how much money you're worth and how to follow a budget. You'll learn what financial documents to keep and how to organize them to make your budgeting easier. Then, you can find out the best ways to borrow, whether you want a new credit card or a mortgage to buy a house. The next chapter will walk you through the basics of investing and review the choices available, based on your goals, how much money you have, and your risk tolerance. The following chapters cover key aspects of your financial life—home ownership, insuring yourself and your property, saving for your kids' college education, planning for retirement, and managing your estate. The appendices offer tips on how to resolve common consumer problems along with a resource list of government agencies, nonprofit groups, and other organizations that can help you. There is also a glossary of common investment terms and a list of books and software if you're interested in doing further reading about any of the topics covered in this book.

WHY SHOULD I BE MY OWN PLANNER?

Having control of your finances is empowering. You will understand your current financial situation and what steps you have to take to reach your future goals. Planning becomes a continuous process; as your life changes—a new job, children, marriage, illness—you will have to evaluate your options and update your plans. Most of all, understanding your finances means that you will have control over your life. If you have a cushion of savings, you may well be able to quit a job you hate and start your own business. Or, if you're determined to retire early and travel around the world, you may want to work harder or start a sideline business in order to accumulate the necessary extra income. The choice can be yours!

CHAPTER 1

ORGANIZE AND BUDGET

You're so hungry that you can practically smell the cookies as you line up the ingredients you'll need. You've made them so many times that you don't even need to have the recipe in front of you. Oops—where are those chocolate chips? As the Boy Scout motto goes, "Be prepared." You should have double-checked your recipe to make sure you had all the ingredients. Going out to the grocery store to buy chips isn't a big deal. However, if the nearest store is an hour's drive, you'll be annoyed.

Preparation—knowing what you need and making sure you have it—is just part of life. Even kids in kindergarten quickly learn that if they forget their lunchbox at home or on the bus, they won't have their peanut butter sandwich.

Preparation is a necessary first step to taking control of your finances. You have to start at the beginning by keeping track of any paperwork related to your finances. If you've paid taxes, you're already familiar with the process of organizing your tax records. Each April, you need to find your pay stubs, W-2 forms, brokerage statements, receipts from charities, bank statements, etc. Perhaps you hand over a shoebox full of paper to your accountant. If your accountant is your brother-in-law, that may be okay.

However, there's more to saving records than just stashing them away. You want to be able to find documents quickly when you need them. If you come home and realize that your house has been broken into, you want to immediately find your home owner's policy without having to search through stacks of paper. Or, if you go to your ATM and find out that your account is overdrawn, you need to review your last bank statement right away.

GETTING ORGANIZED

Generally, it's advisable to keep all receipts and tax records for at least three years. That way, if you're unfortunate enough to be audited, you'll have paperwork to back up your return. You may design a unique style for saving paperwork, depending on issues like availability of storage space and whether or not you're a packrat.

Some records can be thrown out quickly: Unless you work at home and claim deductions for a home office, there's no point saving utility bills year after year. After you pay your credit card bills, you can throw out receipts from the gas station, grocery store, restaurant, etc. However, you may want to save the receipts for high ticket items such as appliances or computers, in case you need to have the item repaired or serviced under a warranty.

Whether you're planning on handling all your finances on your own or you expect to seek help from an accountant, lawyer, or other professional, you should set up some type of filing system to organize your records. Once you set up the system, keeping track of your papers will be effortless, and budgeting and managing your money will be easier. After all, that is why you are reading this book! It doesn't matter what filing system you use, as long as it makes sense to you and other members of your family who will also need to see the papers. You can use an expandable folder with alphabetical headings for categories such as bank, brokerage, credit card, home, insurance, taxes, etc. You might want to have two folders, one for papers you use often and another for documents that you review only once or twice a year. Current bills and pending matters include:

- Credit card bills and statements
- Pay stubs
- Other bills, such as garage, school, insurance, medical, etc.
- Bank and brokerage statements for the current year

Material that you need infrequently includes:

- Tax returns from the past three to five years
- Bank statements and canceled checks
- Employee benefits information
- Health records for you and other family members
- Your will and other documents related to estate planning, such as a letter of instructions and cemetery plot information
- Insurance policies

In addition, you should keep other important paperwork (or in some cases copies) at home as well as in a safe deposit box. These types of papers include your birth certificate, marriage license, passport, home owner's deed, death certificates, etc.

Don't get bogged down in organizing this paperwork. If your office desk looks like a cyclone but you always manage to find the file you need, don't sweat it too much.

If you absolutely hate papers, you might look into a digital organizing system (such as Quicken, by Intuit) to use on your computer. Remember, by keeping track of these papers, you're getting a head start in the process of monitoring your finances and taking control of your money. Once you're organized, you can concentrate on the more important issues, such as how much money you're spending and saving and how you can make your money go farther.

CREATING A BUDGET

When you hear the word budget, you may think of Washington bureaucrats keeping track of the trillions of dollars spent by the government—and the federal budget hasn't been balanced in years! Don't worry, though; establishing your own budget is far easier than figuring out what it costs to run an entire country. Anyone can learn how to keep a budget, even those of you who never balance your checkbook or end up scrambling to finish your taxes very late on April 14.

What is a budget? It is simply a way to keep track of what you spend and what you earn over a specific period of time, such as a week or month. There is no one right or wrong way to budget, so you should use whatever method that enables you to monitor your income and expenses in an easy, painless fashion. If your spending is under control and you have your own investment portfolio, creating a budget may seem like a waste of time. However, even if your spending isn't excessive and you've been able to set aside some of your salary as savings on a regular basis, you should still have a budget.

Let's assume you've just graduated from college and have landed your first job. After several years of part-time jobs, checks from your parents, and endless meals at campus hangouts, your paycheck probably seems like a grand sum. But if you start thinking about what you want to do with your newfound earnings—take that trip to Europe, buy a new car, find an apartment of your own, and, of course, start paying back your college loans—you'll soon realize that you have to devise a plan that will allow you to do these things. Even if you've been working for a while and have a house and children, you're liable to find yourself in financial hot water if you haven't been monitoring your spending.

Writing down all your expenses on paper is an easy way to keep track of what you're spending. If you've ever had to follow a strict diet, you know that putting something down on paper forces you to pay attention. As part of many weight reduction programs, counselors urge you to write down everything you eat and when you consume the food. Keeping this record isn't usually enough incentive to stop you from overindulging with your favorite food, but when you look back at your food diary, you'll inevitably start to recognize your eating patterns; some of you may even start to change your eating habits because you don't want to be embarrassed by your food record.

Likewise, by keeping a written record of your expenses and your earnings, you'll learn more about your spending and your savings habits. Armed with this new knowledge, you can then make positive changes in your finances. You can choose to save more or spend less on discretionary purchases. You can work toward your future goals, such as accumulating money for a down payment on a house or setting aside a nest egg that will enable you to retire early or help pay for your kids' college tuition. You might even be able to buy that red Corvette that you've been dreaming about for years.

If you're still skeptical about the value of a budget, consider the following:

- A budget makes you more aware of your spending and hence can make you a more careful shopper. For example, those of you who live in urban areas might often stop off after work for fresh vegetables to make a salad or, if you've had a particularly trying day, for gourmet takeout. But, you probably also do major grocery shopping at a larger super-market every other week. Add up those nightly bills along with your grocery tab and you'll probably gasp at what you're spending just on food!

- Sticking to a budget can help you avoid major financial crises, such as those created by credit card abuse. When you see on paper what you're actually spending compared to what you're earning, you are more likely to slow down your purchases. Really, it's easy to forget how much you're spending, especially if you and your spouse each pay several different bills.

- Budgets help you and your family work toward specific financial and other goals more successfully. With everyone in your family, including your children, aware of your budget and what is motivating your decisions, they are likely to be more cooperative and involved in the spending and saving process. Family goals such as a new car or a trip to Disney World are bound to be very powerful motivational tools to help you follow your budget.

Goals

Before you sit down with pencil and paper to work on a budget, you should analyze your goals. Think of the financial objectives you want to achieve. You should consider practical goals, such as buying a house or accumulating a certain-size investment portfolio, as well as your dream list. If your child has just started kindergarten, then perhaps one of your goals should be to accumulate enough money in another fifteen years to pay his or her college tuition or at least a portion of the educational expenses. If you're also keen on retiring at age fifty-five and sailing around the world, you should list this as one of your goals, even if you're reasonably certain you would have to win the lottery before you could set sail. It helps if you think of your goals as being short term, intermediate term, or long term. Here's a goal list for the Smith family. Both Mr. and Mrs. Smith currently work, and James Smith is a four year old in full-time day care.

Short Term

Send James to camp next summer.

Take a week-long trip to Disney World.

Buy a computer for the family room.

Intermediate Term

Buy a second car within two to three years.

Build an addition to their house.

Pay off credit card bills.

Figure out how Mrs. Smith can stay home or work part-time when they have a second child.

Long Term

Accumulate $20,000 toward James's college tuition.

Buy a sailboat.

Set aside money to help Mrs. Smith's parents, should they need long-term care.

While you won't be able to determine exactly how much money you will need to achieve the long-term goals, you should be able to make some good estimates based on your specific timetable. For example, if you want to accumulate $20,000 in fifteen years, you know that you have to set aside $1,333 each year for fifteen years. (Actually, you could save less each year, provided you invest the money and it earns some return.)

It will be much easier to determine how much money you will need to save for your short-term and intermediate-term goals. You can find out what a trip to Disney World will cost by calling a travel agent and getting airfare and hotel information. If the trip will cost $2,500 and you want to go in a year, then you have to set aside $208.33 a month toward this vacation. You might even want to set up a worksheet along these lines:

Goal	Total to Save	Date Needed By	Savings Each Month
Vacation	$2,500	Next June (12 months away)	$208.33

Putting It on Paper

The best way to start preparing a budget is to write down all your expenses. If you've resisted setting up a budget, this will be an especially annoying task. However, after you have written down your expenses for several months, you will have a much clearer picture of your expenditures, and you won't have to write down every last purchase, like your morning coffee or a newspaper. That is, provided you have the discipline to modify your spending and savings in order to work toward your goals. Remember, your budget is useless if you simply write down what you spend and what you earn and then put the paper away and never review it. A budget is supposed to give you the freedom that comes with being aware of your spending. You can make your spending decisions based on what you want rather than what you have to do in order to pay off your debts.

To start tracking your spending, get a memo pad that you can carry around with you. Label a page with the day of the week, and write down every purchase you make. Write down everything! Don't assume that you will remember what you spent on Monday if you wait until the next weekend to write it down. Once you start to recognize your spending habits, you'll probably find some big surprises. If you and your spouse both work, you will notice duplicate expenses that were incurred perhaps because you were both too busy or didn't check with each other. How often have you both brought something for dinner on the way home from work? Do you both buy the same magazines or books, not knowing that the other person is also interested in them? Don't worry about who pays the major bills or whether you have separate and joint checking accounts.

Think about what you spend each day on costs such as newspapers, lunch, snacks, etc. Here's a sample list of common expenses:

Public transportation $2.50 (both ways) or Gas $5.00

Newspaper $1.25

Morning coffee/bagel $1.25

Package of gum $.50

Lunch $6.00

Afternoon snack (chips) $.50

Carryout for dinner $15.00

Video rental $4.00

That's only about $30 a day, you may be saying. Yes, and it adds up to an astounding $150 for a five-day work week, and that's just for daily incidentals. Add the cost of theater tickets, more gas, emergency car repairs, medical bills, and whatever else you would have to pay for during a week. Assume that your spouse is spending a similar amount—between the two of you, you're spending more than $300 just to get through Monday to Friday. This is not an outrageous amount of money if your take-home pay for the week is $1,000 or more. But if your salary is less, then you could be headed for trouble.

Carry your memo pad with you, or write down what you spend while you're working on your office calendar and then transfer the amounts to your memo pad. Actually, how you record your spending doesn't matter, as long you include everything. Don't make a production of whipping out your memo pad in front of friends or colleagues if you're easily embarrassed. Just take your notes later. In addition to your daily expenses, you should also write down other weekly and monthly expenses, including grocery bills, health club payments, utility bills, parking fees, as well as any other payments that you have to make regularly, such as your rent or mortgage, insurance premiums, tuition, loans, credit cards bills, etc. Here's a list of the most common expenses you are likely to have:

Rent

Utilities

Insurance (health, home owner's, etc.)

Loans (car, educational, etc.)

Taxes

Commuting expenses

Entertainment (dining out, movies, vacation)

Medical bills (doctor bills, pharmacy expenses)

Food

Clothing

Personal (health club membership, haircuts, etc.)

Miscellaneous

Again, it's important that you not leave anything out. Unlike a diet, where you may lose weight even if you don't tell the truth about what you eat, cheating on your budget is just plain foolish. You'll only increase your chances of ending up deeper in debt or unable to meet your goals. By writing down all your expenses—both the necessary and the optional ones—you'll start to see recurring patterns. You may not be aware of what and how much you're spending each month. You may even wince in pain when you realize how you've been squandering so much of your hard-earned salary!

After a month or two of tracking these expenses, you should have a much better idea of where your money is going. You will be ready to prepare a record of your expenses month to month for a year. You should divide your spending into three key categories: fixed, variable, and miscellaneous. Fixed expenses are the regular payments that you must pay each month, such as your rent or mortgage, premiums, loan payments, etc. Variable expenses are expenses that vary, such as telephone and utility bills. Miscellaneous expenses include almost everything else that you pay for without knowing ahead of time that you'll need it. This category includes gifts, meals, movies, video rentals, etc.

Consider using a worksheet as follows (this worksheet is adapted from *The Consumer Budget Planner,* American Financial Services Association).

If you make certain payments on a quarterly basis, write down each payment and note the month you regularly pay it. If you're unsure when you pay certain bills, refer back to your checkbook for last year and see when you paid various bills and note the amounts. Use these figures as a way to estimate any categories that you haven't yet received bills for. If you're trying to save a set amount each month, put this amount down as if it were a fixed obligation. You should then be able to add up the amount of money you spend each month.

Compare the monthly expenditures to your earnings each month. Prepare a similar month by month worksheet where you can write down your salary along with any interest, dividends, or other income. Use last year's tax returns to estimate this year's earnings. Now, compare the income with your spending worksheet. If you have more money coming in than you're paying out, good for you! You're ready to graduate from Budgeting 101. But if you're in the red, like the government, you have to get cracking on your own version of budget reform.

Item	Average Monthly Expense	Total Year Expense
SHELTER		
Rent or mortgage	1270.46	_____
Property taxes		_____
Property insurance		_____
Maintenance	_____	_____
Gas, oil, electricity	102.87	_____
Telephone	100	_____
Water and sewer	49.50	_____
Other	_____	_____
FOOD		
Groceries	287.49	_____
Meals away from home	_____	_____
Tobacco/alcohol	_____	_____
Other	_____	_____
TRANSPORTATION		
Car payments	_____	_____
Gasoline, oil, etc.	41.13	_____
Maintenance and repair	_____	_____
Auto insurance	54.13	_____
Public transportation	_____	_____
Carpool costs	_____	_____
Taxes and fees	_____	_____
Other	_____	_____
CLOTHING		
New purchases	_____	_____
Dry cleaning/laundry	_____	_____
Mending, repair	_____	_____
Other	_____	_____

Item	Average Monthly Expense	Total Year Expense
HEALTH CARE		
Physicians, dentists	_____	_____
Drugs (including nonprescription)	_____	_____
Health/hospital insurance	_____	_____
Hospital costs	_____	_____
Other	_____	_____
PERSONAL CARE		
Hair care	_____	_____
Toiletries	_____	_____
Personal care appliances	_____	_____
Pocket money allowances	_____	_____
Other	_____	_____
RECREATION		
Vacations	_____	_____
Recreational equipment	_____	_____
Recreational activities	_____	_____
Movies, theater	_____	_____
Parties at home	_____	_____
Newspapers, books, etc.	_____	_____
Club dues	_____	_____
Other	_____	_____
GIFTS AND CONTRIBUTIONS		
Religious/charities	_____	_____
Political causes	_____	_____
Family gifts	_____	_____
Non–family gifts	_____	_____
Holiday gifts	_____	_____
Other	_____	_____

Item	Average Monthly Expense	Total Year Expense
SAVINGS		
Savings accounts	_____	_____
Life insurance	_____	_____
Disability insurance	_____	_____
Investments	_____	_____
Retirement contributions	_____	_____
Other	_____	_____
OBLIGATIONS		
Alimony/child support	_____	_____
Child care	_____	_____
Credit card payments	_____	_____
Other debt payments	_____	_____
EDUCATION		
Education/training expenses	_____	_____
TOTAL EXPENDITURES		_____
- - - - - - - - - - - - - - - - - - -		
INCOME		
All salaries and wages		_____
Average commission income		_____
Average part-time work		_____
Alimony/child support		_____
Dividends/interest		_____
Pensions/Social Security		_____
Other		_____
TOTAL INCOME		_____
TOTAL EXPENDITURES		_____
BALANCE		_____

REDUCE YOUR SPENDING

Even if you have to cut back on your spending, don't panic and think that you can instantly change your habits. After all, you know how hard it is to change your eating habits when you start a diet. First, look back through your expenses. More than half of your spending is devoted to fixed payments. It's unlikely that you can reduce these payments immediately, so you have to look to reduce your spending in the other categories, which you have control over. Also, as you review your spending, consider whether some of the expenses were unusual or related to special events. For example, if you spent $8,000 on entertainment, was it because you had parties for your daughter's engagement, your twenty-fifth wedding anniversary, and your son's high school graduation? Presumably, these are one-time events, and you can drastically reduce the amount of money you spend on entertainment for the next year or so.

Continue to look for ways to reduce your spending. Even if you're fairly certain that your salary will increase or you'll get a year-end bonus, you shouldn't assume that your income will increase sufficiently to cover all your spending. Instead, you should focus on ways to cut back on your spending:

- Look for savings on clothing and groceries by joining a warehouse club, buying fruits and vegetables at a food co-op, etc.
- See if your utilities company offers a savings program or will come to your home for a free inspection to see whether you can take advantage of a cost savings program.
- Instead of buying videos or renting from a video store, see if your local library rents them for free.
- Look for discount/coupon programs to use at local restaurants, hotels, and movie theaters.
- Comparison-shop before you make major purchases such as appliances.

You should include your whole family in making these changes. Obviously, if your children are small, they may not be responsible directly for the family spending. However, you should start teaching your children about budgeting and explain that they can't always have everything that they want. They have to save up for certain treats or decide which of several luxury items they want the most. And, if your children are old enough to manage their own spending—whether it's money you give them as allowance or money they earn from part-time jobs—you should encourage them to spend more prudently as well. For example, see if your teen can buy those designer jeans when they go on sale rather than the day the store gets them in his or her size.

If you need more hints on cutting back your spending, several helpful newsletters offer a variety of tips on saving more and spending less. Among these publications are:

- *The Pocket Change Investor* (P. O. Box 78, Elizaville, NY 12523): two years/eight issues, $19.95

- *Cheapskate Monthly* (P. O. Box 2135, Paramount, CA 90723): one year/twelve issues, $15.95

- *The Penny Pincher* (P. O. Box 809, Kings Park, NY 11754): one year/twelve issues, $15

- *$ensible $aver Publications* (6488 Victory Drive, Acworth, GA 30102): one year/twelve issues, $24.95

As you make these changes in your spending, continue to keep careful track of your expenses on paper. Hopefully, you will establish new habits, and, in a short while, you won't have to monitor yourself so closely. The aim, after all, is to establish a reasonable budget that you will be able to follow. Then, you should update and alter your budget once or twice a year or when your financial circumstances change—if you get a new job, have a new child, or have other major life changes.

If you're completely exasperated with the notion of budgeting, don't despair. If you're comfortable using a computer, several excellent programs are available to help track your spending. Among these are:

- Kiplinger's CA Simply Money (Computer Associates; 800-322-8621): This program enables you to monitor all your investments and savings and includes tips on smarter financial moves.

- Quicken (Intuit; 800-624-8742): This program helps you track your spending, savings, and investments and also lets you pay your bills on-line.

If you still have trouble keeping your savings on track, look for little tricks that limit your access to cash. For example, if your employer has direct deposit, use it to have your paycheck put directly into a bank or mutual fund account. That way, you'll know the money is in the bank, hopefully for savings, rather than the idle spending you might do if you simply cashed your paycheck. And, if you still have difficulty setting aside money to pay your bills, you could resort to the old-fashioned budgeting that some of your grandparents practiced—the envelope method. You cash your paycheck or take a portion of it and put money aside in separate envelopes for the bills you will need to pay that month, including rent, insurance, loans, etc. Put aside the envelopes and then mail them immediately before the due date. This isn't the most practical way for you to take control of your finances, but some people do find it helpful.

As you sort through your spending and saving, remember the point of this exercise: A budget is supposed to help you achieve your financial goals and dreams. It's important to keep these goals in mind, especially if you have to cut back in certain areas. Obviously, you don't want to alarm your children unnecessarily, but you should be able to talk to them about your choices. Explain that in order to save money to buy a new car, you won't be able to eat out as frequently. Or, if you buy a new house, you'll have to take a car trip instead of flying to California for your vacation.

Savings: Pay Yourself First

One of the most important fixed expenses is savings. While you may not consider this a fixed expense since you're paying yourself, regularly setting aside money should be as much of a priority as paying your other bills. Regularly saving a portion of your salary is the smartest financial move you will ever make. You should aim to save 5 percent of your salary and gradually increase this percentage to 10 percent of your take-home pay. This may seem daunting as you try to juggle your other payments, but you should be working toward this sum. Of course, there will be times when you will not be able to set aside money because of other obligations. That's all right, but you should never relegate savings to a miscellaneous and irregular payment.

You should also aim to have a savings cushion of three to six months of your living expenses. This is money that should be in a savings account or other short-term account where you will have easy access to your money. This is an emergency account, in case you or your spouse is unable to work or you otherwise suffer a disaster.

A Balance Sheet: What You Have and What You Owe

Your next step is preparing a personal balance sheet. This is simply a list of all your assets and liabilities. Again, by putting this data on paper, you become more focused on your finances. While some accountants might ask that you prepare a more precise breakdown of all your debts and assets, here are the main categories to include in your balance sheet.

Assets

Savings: bank liquid and checking accounts

Investments: stocks, mutual funds

IRA and other retirement accounts

Life insurance: cash value of policy

Home

Car(s)

Personal items, such as jewelry, antiques, and any collections

Liabilities

Home mortgage

Home equity loan

Car loan(s)

Other debt, including credit card(s)

Child care expenses

To determine your net worth, add up the assets and subtract your liabilities. You should use market value or current appraisals for your home, car, or jewelry—in other words, the value of these items, if you were to sell them, is what they are worth. Once you know your net worth—be it positive or negative—you will then have to review both your financial goals and your budget. It's obvious that if your liabilities far exceed your assets, then you will have to make some drastic and immediate changes both in your spending and your lifestyle generally. On the other hand, if the balance sheet is tilted in your favor, you may be able to push up the timetable for some of your long-term goals.

Like your budget and your goals, your net worth will change over time. What is important is for you to control the direction in which it moves. You do that first by creating a realistic budget that you can follow. Then, you should work toward making the smartest financial decisions you can in other areas of your life that will be reflected in your net worth. By following the advice that follows on buying and selling your home, reducing your credit card debt, and making the best investment decisions you can, you'll be headed down the yellow brick road of financial security.

CHAPTER 2

CREDIT

What happens when your eight year old asks you for some overpriced toy that you don't really want to buy? You tell your child that he or she can get the money only by doing some household chores. You will fork over the $50 if your child's bed is made every morning for a month or if the dog is walked before dinner. The cost of the $50 to your child becomes the time and effort involved in doing the requisite chore. On the other hand, when you borrow money, *your* cost is the interest charged by the bank, credit card issuer, or lending institution. You may intend to borrow, say, $500, but you'll end up paying more than $500.

It's very hard to resist the appeal and advantages of credit. After all, it's so difficult to make all your monthly expenses and still have money available to buy a car, take a vacation, or perhaps even to pay for other necessary expenses. You're constantly solicited through the mail, in newspaper ads, and on television. It doesn't matter whether you're a recent college graduate or someone who has had credit problems. You're bound to get some nifty credit card offer that you'll accept. It's no surprise, then, that Americans have become addicted to credit cards. Total credit card debt is well over $300 billion each year. The average American carries nine credit cards in his or her wallet. And nearly half of all credit card holders maintain an average monthly balance of $1,600 a month.

YOUR CREDIT OUTLOOK

When those credit card bills come in, you either blissfully put them aside or make the minimum payments. You may not even know how much you're charging and how much you owe on your various credit cards. Somehow, having a running balance on your cards doesn't seem to matter much. You may not think that being heavily in debt is a big deal. This is a change from an earlier culture: If you reneged on a debt in ancient Rome, you had two choices— death or becoming a slave to the person to whom you owed money! While you're not facing personal indenture, credit problems can be overwhelming. Last year, some 700,000 people sought credit counseling from a nonprofit organization, Consumer Credit Counseling Service (CCCS).

It's crucial that you get a complete picture of your credit situation. Sit down and make a list of all your debts. Don't just think of the larger obligations, such as your mortgage. List all your credit cards, including your department store charges. Include all other obligations, whether you pay them monthly, weekly, or annually, such as student loans, car loans, etc. Once you make this list, note the outstanding balances on each item of credit. Then, sit back and have a cup of coffee or a cold drink. You deserve a break. Seriously, the first step in mastering your use of credit is to know exactly how much money you have borrowed and how much in interest you're paying on this money.

ANALYZE YOUR CREDIT SOURCES

First, some simple definitions. There are two types of credit: secured and unsecured. Secured credit, such as your mortgage or your car loan, means that if you fail to pay, the creditor can take your home or your car. The credit is "secured" by what you have purchased with the loan. Often, furniture purchased on credit is also secured. The more common unsecured credit is that on your credit cards or line of credit at the bank. This form of credit usually costs more—that is, it comes with a higher interest rate—because nothing is securing the loan.

With the proliferation of new credit card issuers as well as tantalizing deals with airlines, long-distance phone carriers, car companies, and other partnerships, it's not unusual for you to use several different cards to take advantage of the extra cardholder benefits. However, you are paying dearly for the use of these cards. The average interest rate on credit cards is 17.73 percent, and most Americans carry a balance of $1,600. With these figures, if you only made the minimum monthly payment on your card, it would take about fifteen years to pay down your balance, and you would have paid almost double your balance in interest payments alone!

If you're really a credit junkie (see section following), then you will have to take drastic action. Some advisors say you should cut up all your credit cards except for one to use in emergencies. Others suggest you keep your cards in some inaccessible place until you have repaid the lion's share of your outstanding balance. It's up to you—you know your own habits and how comfortable you are with your spending. But you should start to reduce your credit

card debt and stop using cards with the highest interest
rates as soon as possible.

You should carefully review your credit card statements and agreements so that you understand exactly
what you are paying in interest. You should also compare
the following features:

Grace period   The grace period is the time from
when you make your purchases to when your bill is
due. The ideal card has a long grace period so that
you're not paying interest immediately on making
your purchase.

Annual percentage rate (APR)   This is the interest rate charged by the bank or credit card issuer.
The APR can be a fixed rate adjusted annually or
when other indices such as the prime rate change.
Obviously, you want a card with the lowest possible
interest rate. For a list of low interest rate cards,
contact the nonprofit BankCard Holders of America
(703-389-5445; $4) or get CardTrack (800-344-7714)
published by RAM Research. Lists of these cards
also appear regularly in *Money, Kiplinger's,* and
other publications.

Finance charges   Finance charges are calculated
in several ways. Usually, the credit card company
considers your average daily balance, which is a total
of the daily balances each month divided by the total
number of days in the month. Another method is
to take the balance for one or two billing cycles. Try to
find a card that takes into account the current cycle
balance only.

Annual fees   Fees range from zero to $35 over a
given year. Usually, when you pay a higher fee, you
have a higher credit limit. That is, you can borrow
more each month. Regardless of the interest rate and
other features of a credit card, you should pay the low-

est possible annual fee. BankCard Holders of America publishes a list of no-fee and low-fee cards. Sometimes, you can negotiate with your credit card issuer and explain that you're canceling your card unless you can pay a lower fee.

Minimum payment Each month, you are required to make a certain payment specified on the bill. Depending on the card, the minimum payment is usually less than 3 percent of the balance owed. You can, of course, pay the entire balance, but you must make at least the minimum payment. Obviously, you will owe interest on anything remaining on your balance.

Remember, too, that certain cards such as American Express, which feature an annual fee, require that you pay off your balance in full each month. This can be a good option in the long run, because there is no interest. If you use your card frequently for travel or business and have the discipline to pay off your bill each month, then you should use one of these cards.

ESTABLISHING A CREDIT HISTORY

If you're one of the few Americans who doesn't have a credit card, you have several ways to build up your credit. One option is a secured credit card. This card operates like any other credit card except that it is secured by a bank deposit.

A better option is to take out a small bank loan and repay it on time. If you've never used credit, taking out a loan may seem foolish. However, to get credit, you have to establish that you are a good credit risk. Once you have repaid your loan, you will have established a credit history and could then apply for an unsecured card.

CREDIT REPORTS

For a long time, the credit approval process seemed to be a big mystery, but today it is simpler to find out why you've been rejected for a loan or credit card. While reading credit reports is still a bit more difficult than reviewing your checking statement, recent revisions to the Fair Credit Reporting Act now make it easier for you to check and correct your credit report. If your loan or insurance application is rejected, you've been turned down for a credit card within the past thirty days, you are unemployed, or you have been a victim of credit fraud, you can get a free copy of your credit report. Furthermore, one of the largest credit reporting agencies, TRW, will provide one free copy of a credit report to all consumers annually (to get this report, write to TRW at the address listed later in this chapter).

Requesting Your Report

It is important when you request your credit report to include all spellings of your name (including maiden and married names, if applicable) as well as your Social Security number, since this is how the credit records are kept. If you and your spouse share credit cards or have cosigned loans, you should include your spouse's full name and his or her Social Security number. When you're writing for a report, also include your birth date, all home addresses for the previous five years, and a copy of your driver's license or of a utility bill that lists your address. If you're writing because you've been turned down for credit, include a copy of the rejection. And don't forget to sign your request.

Reviewing and Correcting Your Report

Although there is a lot of industry jargon on your credit report, you are looking for basic information. Make sure your name, birth date, and Social Security number are accurate. Then review your credit use. You'll see an indication of when you first began using a credit card followed by check marks, which indicate your payment of the bill. If you have missed one or more payments, this is indicated on the credit report.

If you see errors on your credit report, you should immediately write a letter (consider sending it by certified mail) to the three leading credit bureaus:

- TRW (P. O. Box 2350, Chatsworth, CA 91313-2350; 800-682-7654)

- Equifax Credit Information Services (P. O. Box 105873, Atlanta, GA 30348; 800-685-1111)

- Trans Union Corporation (P. O. Box 390, Springfield, PA 19064-0390; 800-851-2674)

You should also write to the creditor that supplied the information to the credit bureau. The letter should include your full name, address, birth date, and Social Security number. The credit bureau that originally printed the error must respond to you within thirty days. If you are dissatisfied with the response, you can contact the creditor directly. Write a letter to the creditor, saying that under the Fair Credit Reporting Act this information should be removed from your record and ask that they contact the credit agency to change your records.

You do have certain rights: delinquent payments, even an outstanding balance that has not been paid, from more than seven years ago cannot be kept on your record. After you've contacted the creditor, you should again check your credit report within three to six months to make sure it is accurate. If the creditor refuses to make the correction, you can sue the creditor.

If your report shows other outstanding recent debts, you should contact the individual creditors and say that you want to work out a payment schedule. Write the specific repayment schedule you're proposing and ask that the creditor sign the letter and send it back to you. This procedure can be followed whether you are repaying a bill in full or making partial payment. Again, it's up to you to check that the creditor has provided the information about repayment to the credit agency. Recently it has been required that all credit bureaus establish toll-free phone numbers for your convenience (see previous listings).

Don't Overdo It

Even if you don't abuse credit cards, it's not a good idea to have too many of them. For example, if you have a credit card with a $10,000 line of credit, then this card will be listed on your credit report. You may have several of these cards. Then, when you apply for a new loan, perhaps for a car, the credit issuers will look at your credit history and may say that you have too much credit. Likewise, if you have cards that you no longer use, call up the credit card issuers and have the cards canceled. Then, when you check your credit reports, make certain that the cards have in fact been canceled and no longer show up on your credit report as active.

Sometimes, just using a little self-control can prevent you from abusing your credit. For example, during the year-end holidays, credit card issuers frequently advertise "Make no payment until . . ." offers. This may sound inviting, but make sure you read the fine print. Almost always, interest charges will still be accruing. If you find that you can't live without your credit cards and your charging isn't out of control, then you should shop for the least expensive cards. Switch to a card with a lower interest rate or find a card with no annual fee. Or, assuming you have more than a six-month cushion in your savings account, you might use your savings to pay off your credit card bills. This strategy may make you somewhat uncomfortable, but remember, your savings account is probably only earning 2 percent or 3 percent interest while you're paying between 15 percent and 20 percent on your credit card bill. Other helpful strategies can be found in publications from the BankCard Holders of America.

HOW MUCH CREDIT SHOULD YOU HAVE?

A good rule of thumb is that all your outstanding debt— credit card, mortgage, etc.—should not be more than 20 percent of your take-home pay. This is referred to as your debt-to-income ratio. Look at your monthly income compared to your monthly debts. You want this ratio to be less than 20 percent. If the ratio is less than 20 percent but much of this debt is new, you should only acquire new debt if absolutely necessary. If the ratio exceeds 20 percent, you should start to worry. And, unfortunately, if it approaches 30 percent, you may be in real trouble (remember, though, this is a rough calculation and doesn't take into account your other assets).

Are You a Credit Junkie?

You're probably well aware if you're in over your head. Here are the most common warning signs of a credit junkie:

- You frequently juggle payments, alternating months of paying the various credit card companies.
- Creditors are calling you.
- You only make the minimum payments on your cards.
- You keep getting new cards.

If you're already in trouble, then sticking your head in the sand will only make your problems worse. You have to contact the creditors and say that you know you're over-extended and you want to work out a repayment plan. If you're really overwhelmed and want someone else to help you work out a payment plan, you should consult a credit counselor. The best are no-cost or low-cost, such as those run by the Consumer Credit Counseling Service (800-388-2227). There are more than 1,000 CCCS offices around the country. You will meet with a counselor who will examine all your debt and then contact your creditors to work out a repayment plan. Not surprisingly, most credit card issuers would like to be paid, so many will be flexible and agree to a repayment schedule. However, it is up to you to keep up your end of the bargain and make these regular payments. If you find the repayment schedule a burden, due to a personal reason such as health problems or job loss, then you should again contact the creditor and explain the extenuating circumstances.

A word of caution: The Federal Trade Commission (FTC) has found that credit repair clinics promising to "fix" bad credit reports are often scams. Before signing on with any credit repair company, check with your local Better Business Bureau, Consumer Affairs Department or Attorney General's Office to make sure that no complaints have been filed against the company.

Remember, too, that you have rights under the federal Fair Debt Collection Practices Act. Debt collectors must send you a written notice of how much and to whom you owe money as well as who to contact if you dispute the debt. If you contact a creditor in writing to dispute the debt, you can't be contacted by the debt collector again unless there is proof of the debt. Collection agents can't threaten you, call you at odd hours, or attempt to garnish wages or property without ample notice. For more information on your rights under this act, call the Federal Trade Commission (202-326-3650) for the *Fair Debt Collection* brochure.

BANKRUPTCY

If you think bankruptcy sounds like a nice and easy out, think again. While many people do choose this alternative, you shouldn't consider it except as your last resort when you've exhausted all other steps to get your spending under control. Once you have declared bankruptcy, it will be difficult for you to get any credit in the future. You may not be able to borrow money to buy a car, purchase a house, or pay for your kids' college education. Also, bankruptcy doesn't absolve you from certain obligations, including alimony and child support payments, student loans, and taxes.

There are two types of bankruptcy for individuals: Chapter 7 and Chapter 13. Chapter 13 is the less drastic of the two bankruptcies. Under this plan, you are not discharging all your debts but rather agreeing to make specific repayments over a certain period of time. You file Chapter 13 in a U.S. District court; the court listens and has to agree to your terms to repay your debts over a three-year period. While Chapter 13 bankruptcy does remain on your credit records for seven years, it does not preclude your getting some credit in the future.

On the other hand, Chapter 7 remains on your credit record for ten years. Under this plan, all your debts with the exception of alimony, taxes, etc. are discharged, and everything you own (except for a home or car or some household effects, depending on where you live) is sold to pay off your creditors. This is a very drastic step. It can be difficult, if not impossible, for you to get credit in the future, even after the bankruptcy is removed from your credit records.

LOANS

Loans are another part of the credit picture. If you know that you will have to borrow money in order to make a major purchase, spend some time thinking about how badly you want or need the item. When you take out a loan, you will always end up paying more than the purchase price. If, for instance, you're buying a car in part because of the low prices and dealer rebates, proceed with caution. Your final cost is likely to be far higher than you anticipate. If you borrow, say, $2,000 from the dealer or a bank, then depending on the interest rate, your final cost for the car will be somewhere between $2,500 and $3,500. Multiply the amount you're borrowing by the interest rate—say for a house or college education—and you can see how much interest adds to your total debt. Among the various types of loans available:

Personal loans Available from banks and credit unions, these loans are made for almost any purpose for amounts from $2,000 to $25,000. Interest on these loans is no longer deductible, and interest rates will range greatly. Generally, if your loan is secured—by a bank account or CD—you can get a slightly lower interest rate. You should shop around when you're applying for a personal loan, although you will usually do best seeking a loan from a bank or institution where you already have accounts or other business. Sometimes, you can establish a line of credit on a personal loan, not unlike lines of credit commonly associated with home equity loans. With a line of credit, you have access to the loan when you need it—say if you expect to pay bills in the coming months for repairs to a home or car.

Auto loans One of the most common types of loan taken out today is the car loan. And, unfortunately for you, it's all too easy to be confused by the ads from car dealers and banks. It's important that you separate the process of shopping for a particular car with shopping for a car loan. While a car dealer might be quick to quote you a "low monthly payment" price that includes the price of a car combined with the loan, you should insist on finding out the purchase price of the car and then the terms of any loan available through the dealer. Once you know the price of the car, you can comparison-shop for a loan at local banks. Don't forget that cars lose their value over time, so you should not take out a car loan for longer than five years, or else you'll owe more on the loan than the car is worth. Also, you should put down at least a 20 percent down payment, or else you'll pay a higher interest rate.

Mortgages   Since buying a home is likely to be the most major purchase of your adult life, you should search for a mortgage very carefully. There are now new twists on the basic mortgages. The two basic types are fixed rate and variable rate. A fixed mortgage is one that you take out for a specified length of time—generally fifteen or thirty years at a set rate for the entire term of the mortgage. Recently, average thirty-year fixed rates were 9.25 percent. Variable mortgages feature interest rates that fluctuate according to other indices such as the Treasury rate. The appeal of variable-rate mortgages is the low initial rate, which you pay for six months or one year. Then, the rate is usually adjusted up or down once a year.

If you don't stick to a budget or if your income varies greatly from year to year, variable-rate mortgages may not be right for you (if, in fact, you qualify for one), because you could find yourself hard-pressed to keep up the payments when they rise. On the other hand, if you're not planning to stay in your house for more than three to five years, you should consider a variable-rate mortgage. You could save on your interest costs dramatically. Another type of loan is the convertible, really a hybrid of fixed and variable. This type of loan starts off as an adjustable-rate mortgage and then switches to a fixed rate somewhere from year three to five. (For more on mortgages, see chapter 4.)

Home equity loans   These loans have remained quite attractive because of their tax advantage. You can deduct interest on home loans up to $100,000 regardless of what you use the loan for. So, although the loans were intended to help with expansion or repairs, there's nothing to stop you from using the loan for other reasons. However, there's one major drawback to taking out a home equity loan: if you default and can't pay back the loan, you could lose your home. With your home as security, it's important that you take out a home equity loan for a real purpose and not just to make frivolous purchases.

Usually, you can borrow up to 80 percent of the value of your home, excluding the balance of any mortgage you already have on the house. You can usually take the loan as a fixed amount or have a line of credit to draw upon when you need the money. When you take out a home equity loan, you will have to pay some of the same costs you would with a mortgage, including application fee (generally $100, which is probably nonrefundable), closing costs such as title search and bank documents, and annual fees. Look for loans with interest rates that don't increase by more than two points a year or five points over the life of the loan.

CHAPTER 3

INVEST YOUR WAY TO A WINNING FUTURE

A quick look at the headlines in the business section of your local newspaper may send you scurrying around your house to find a new hiding place for any extra cash you have. One day, interest rates are soaring; the next week, they drop off. Overseas markets are supposed to be flourishing, but then the Mexican economy falls apart. You work way too hard for your money to watch it disappear into investments that you don't fully understand and can't easily monitor. Even skilled professionals cannot make absolutely accurate predictions about economic conditions. After all, how many people were prepared for the crash of October 1987?

So, why should you invest? If you've learned anything from reading this book so far, it's that you must be master of your money. Whether you want to buy a new house, take a vacation, or dramatically change your lifestyle, it's up to you to get control of your finances so you're able to work toward your goal. It's not always a simple task, given the ever-increasing types of investments, bank accounts, re-tirement plans, and other financial services products. There is good news, though, about these new products: You have more options from which to select, even if you only have relatively small sums of money to invest. Once you have a firm grip on the basics—establishing a budget, maintaining an emergency fund, getting sufficient insur-ance coverage—you can then begin exploring the world of investments.

INVESTING MEANS BEATING THE RATE OF INFLATION

If your money is in a savings account, you are not in-vesting for your future.

Investing is the only way you'll keep ahead of inflation, which is currently about 3 percent. If you've already trans-formed yourself from a credit junkie to a careful saver who is regularly putting money into a bank account—terrific! You've taken the most valuable first step in managing your money. However, don't assume that putting your cash into an account where it earns 2 percent to 3 percent in-terest means you've made a sound investment decision. In fact, over time, you would actually lose money, because your account holdings wouldn't keep up with inflation. You have to get over your fears, worries, memories of the De-pression, or whatever else keeps you from investing. Just do it—start to invest.

Well, don't do it immediately. Read this chapter and do some research first. Don't put any of your money into an in-vestment before you understand its advantages and disad-vantages. You won't learn everything about the investment world in this chapter. But you will acquire a working knowledge of the most common types of investments, how to figure out which investment is best suited to your needs, and how to evaluate your tolerance for risk. With your new-found understanding of the investment options, along with your perceptions of your own finances, you will be able to make informed investment decisions.

You may want to get some help—from a planner or broker—but you should do your own homework. Don't ever be strong-armed by a fast-talking salesperson into investing in something that you don't fully understand. Be especially wary if someone offers you the investment dream of a lifetime that's only available for a limited time. That's exactly the type of investment that you should avoid. Other investment opportunities in real estate or complex securities are too risky for most of you. Also, some investments that require large outlays of cash, such as collectibles, silver, or artwork, are probably not right for your needs, especially if you're a fledgling investor. Don't worry, though, because there are many other investment opportunities that don't require large amounts of money and are much less volatile.

PLAN YOUR STRATEGY TODAY

You can be a cautious investor, but the sooner you start investing, the more money you will accumulate to meet your goals.

You feel comfortable because most of your money is in a bank account. That means you're not taking any risk. Your money, up to $100,000 in each bank in which you have an account, is insured by the Federal Deposit Insurance Corporation (FDIC). When you close your account, you'll get back whatever money you put into the account along with the amount of interest your deposits have earned. This is

an investment with zero risk. Another investment with
very low risk is U.S. savings bonds. The interest that your
savings bond will earn is tied to the average yield of Treasury securities. The bond's interest rate is adjusted periodically, and since it's unlikely that you will know what
the interest rate of the five-year Treasury note is, you certainly won't be able to predict what your savings bond will
earn. But your original investment—what you paid for the
bond—is 100 percent safe. If you pay $500 for the bond,
you will always get back that $500. What varies is how
much additional money in interest the bond will earn.

However, if you want to stay well ahead of inflation
and keep your portfolio growing, you simply have to take
some risks. You have probably heard about the new
pyramid approach to eating: The bottom of the pyramid
is for pasta, grains, fruits, and vegetables—the healthy
food that you should be consuming. At the top of the
pyramid are fats and meats, which you're advised to eat
only occasionally. You can also view your investments in
a pyramid fashion: The riskiest investments—junk
bonds, real estate, and gold—are at the top of the pyramid. Depending on the state of your finances, you should
have none or only a small percentage of your holdings in
these very speculative investments. At the bottom of the
pyramid are risk-free investments, such as savings
bonds, savings accounts, and certificates of deposit
(CDs). The middle of the pyramid contains low and moderate risk investments, such as mutual funds, government bonds, and blue-chip stocks (holdings from the
thirty companies whose stock comprise the Dow Jones
Industrial Average). The most conservative investor
would have all of his or her holdings at the bottom of the
pyramid, and these portfolios wouldn't grow much over
time. If you're still conservative but want more return
on your money, you will keep most of your holdings in
the middle of the pyramid.

Your Risk Comfort Zone

Some advisors have designed clever surveys to help you understand your capacity for risk taking. These surveys can be entertaining and helpful, especially if you fill them out with a spouse or friend who doesn't share your values and attitude toward money. But you don't have to complete one of these questionnaires in order to start investing. Chances are, you know how you feel about money and how well you handle it. Do you limit yourself to quarter slot machines, or can you easily blow several thousand dollars playing poker, even though you can ill afford to lose the money? Are you content to lose an occasional $10 in the football pool at the office? The simplest way to gauge your tolerance for risk is to ask yourself whether you would still be able to sleep comfortably at night if you made a particular investment.

For example, if you hear the economic forecast on the evening news, will you count sheep as you wonder whether your stocks are going to take a nose-dive? Or, if you see everyone rushing to try a new product in the grocery store, will you have nightmares over your recent purchase of stock in a competitor's company? You probably have ample reasons enough to lie awake at night; don't add investments to your list of worries. Aim to find the investment that is most appropriate to your needs and one that you will be able to hold onto for a period of time until your needs change and/or the investment is no longer right for you.

Other Considerations

In addition to your tolerance for risk, there are several other key factors you must consider before formulating your investment strategy:

The purpose of your investment   Your investments should enable you to meet your personal and financial goals. Know what you are investing for, whether it's early retirement, a house, or paying for your kids' college education.

Time horizon   You need to have a clear notion of how long you can invest your money. Obviously, if you expect you'll need the money in a year or two, you shouldn't select an investment that is intended for long-term growth. Remember, too, that you may be hit with early withdrawal penalties and other fees if you have to get out of an investment early. On the other hand, if you're investing for a long-term goal, then you should look to get the highest rate of return. And you should be willing to select slightly riskier investments, because in the long run, your portfolio will withstand both upturns and downturns in the economy.

Your involvement   How active an investor do you intend to be? You may simply want to find a broker whose opinion you trust, then rely on his or her recommendations. On the other hand, if you have the time and inclination, you can do much of your own homework by reading magazines, business sections of newspapers, and personal finance newsletters. If you've researched various investments, narrowed down your choices, and finally selected one, you can then buy stocks from a discount broker or mutual funds directly from the company and save on commission fees.

Short term needs   If you're retired or are working part-time, you may need an investment that will provide a steady income in the form of dividends.

Before making a choice, you should also be prepared to evaluate the following three factors, which are intrinsic to all investments:

Safety Is your investment guaranteed, as with U.S. savings bonds, or can it decline in value so that you lose whatever money you've invested, as with real estate?

Liquidity How easy is it for you get back your initial investment? Will you have to find a buyer for your investment? Will you lose money by getting out before a certain period of time?

Return This is the rate at which you can make money on your investment. You should look for a return that outpaces inflation, which has been averaging around 3 percent a year.

DIVERSIFY, DIVERSIFY, DIVERSIFY!

Put your money into different investments — those that differ by industry, time period, and rate of return.

The old adage, "Don't put all your eggs in one basket" is probably the best investment advice for everyone. Even so-called Wall Street gurus have difficulty devising winning strategies some of the time. You can wade through government forecasts about the economy or look at statistics about the direction of interest rates and periods of inflation over the past decade. Still, even if you were able to fathom all this data, you would need a crystal ball to see how investments will perform in the future.

Don't believe anyone who says he or she has "a 100 percent guaranteed winning investment." They don't exist. That's why you should spread your eggs around. Put your money into different types of investments as well as investments of varying time duration. If you've made one wrong pick, you won't lose everything, because you've got investments in other vehicles. And if you want to switch your investments to catch movement in the economy, all your money won't be locked into another investment. This is what diversification means: you are spreading out your risk by selecting several investments.

Don't assume that you have to have accumulated a large sum of money before you can start to invest. In fact, you can start off with a modest sum of money—whatever is left after you have paid your monthly bills and kept up your emergency fund. Because of compounding, even a small amount of money will quickly accumulate. Assume that you can put aside $100 every year. How much could you save over time, assuming your money will earn interest that is compounded annually?

Interest Rate	Years			
	5	10	15	20
8%	$587	$1,318	$2,328	$3,679
10%	611	1,594	3,177	5,727
12%	635	1,755	3,728	7,205

These totals may not seem like a lot, considering that inflation over time will also diminish the value of your savings. But most of you save far more than $100 each year. Also, if your money is compounded more frequently, say quarterly or monthly, you'll earn even more. To estimate how much you can save with the impact of compounding, use the rule of seventy-two. Divide seventy-two by the interest rate your money is earning. The answer is the number of years it will take for your money to double. For example, if your money is earning 12 percent, it will take six years for it to double in value.

Start Simple

Select investments that you understand.

A very popular investment choice right now is mutual funds, in which your money is pooled with money from other investors. This money is then invested by a professional money manager. Although mutual funds may be the "sexy" investment of the '90s, you shouldn't overlook other conservative investments such as Treasury notes and certificates of deposit (CDs) that may be more appropriate to your needs. Although your return will probably not be as much as you would earn with other investments such as stocks, these are still good places for your money, especially if you anticipate needing the money to make a major purchase, such as a house or car, in the not-too-distant future. Among these investments:

Certificates of deposit   These accounts are available at banks and other financial institutions. You leave on deposit a set amount of money—ranging from $500 to as much as $25,000—for a specified period of time. You can get a one-month, three-month, or six-month CD, and so on, up through several-year terms. Each deposit up to $100,000 per bank is insured by the FDIC. The interest rates on CDs are usually tied to the rate of Treasury bills and can vary greatly. Lately, though, they have been higher than over the past few years. For example, in the spring of 1995, the average annual yield on a six-month CD was 4.76 percent; the average yield on a one-year CD was 5.70 percent.

Generally, the longer the term, the higher the interest rate. You have to limit your options to what's available at your local bank. Look at a financial publication, such as *Money* or *Kiplinger's*, which regularly list CDs available at banks around the country. Read the fine print carefully so you know exactly what you will earn over the term of the CD. Make sure that you don't lock yourself into a long-term CD if there's any chance that you will need the money before the CD matures. Penalties for early withdrawal can be steep. A good strategy is to buy several smaller CDs of varying maturities such as six months, one year, or eighteen months. That way, when one CD matures, you can compare interest rates at that time and decide whether to put the money back into a CD or select another investment that will earn a higher return.

You can get also buy a CD from a broker. Some brokers have access to banks that you would not know about. However, you will have to pay a commission on your transaction. Compare the interest rate and what you would earn over the term of the CD along with the fee to what you could get on your own.

Treasury issues   Risk-free securities can be bought from the U.S. government, although the minimum amounts to buy these bills or notes are higher than for CDs. You can buy these government issues through a broker, although you will pay a commission ranging from $25 to $100, or directly from the government. To buy a Treasury issue, you should get an application from a Federal Reserve bank or branch. (For a list of these banks, call the Bureau of Public Debt at 202-874-4000, extension 3.) By completing the application, you are spelling out at what price you are willing to bid for the issue; the securities are auctioned regularly by the Treasury Department. The Treasury takes your check and opens a Treasury direct account.

The minimum amount for getting a T-note is $1,000; the minimum amount for a T-bill is $10,000. You should buy directly from the government when you plan to hold the securities until their maturity date. If you have to sell a Treasury issue prior to maturity, you will have to go to a broker or bank and pay a commission. Recent yields on Treasury securities: 6.64 percent for one-year T-bills; 7.35 percent for five-year T-notes.

Money market funds   These funds, available from mutual fund companies, are best for putting aside relatively small amounts of money that you anticipate needing in the near future. You can get your money out without paying withdrawal penalties or fees. Recent money market fund rates were slightly higher than six-month CD rates, averaging 5.43 percent. One caution: Money market funds are not insured as are bank money market funds, which earn much lower rates.

Savings bonds   Savings bonds continue to be a very popular investment vehicle. They are easy to buy and can be purchased for very small amounts of money; a $50 bond is purchased for $25; a $500 bond is bought for $250 and so on. Savings bonds can be a useful investment strategy for college savings (see chapter 6), although recent changes in how interest rates are set for the bonds make them somewhat less attractive than in the past. There used to be a 4 percent minimum interest rate on bonds, but for all bonds bought after May 1, 1995, the interest rate will be set every six months. For the first five years, the interest rate will be 85 percent of the average yield on six-month Treasury bills and, after that, 85 percent of the average interest rate on five-year Treasury notes.

Depending on your tax bracket, you may still be interested in savings bonds. You pay no state or local tax on the interest. Plus, you have the option of paying your federal tax each year or, when the bonds mature, when you cash them in or give them away.

Mutual Funds

While you may be tempted to buy individual shares of stock with the money you've earmarked for investing, stocks are not the best choice for a fledgling investor. Stocks are generally sold in round lots of fifty or one hundred shares. When you buy a small number of shares, you will have to pay a higher commission to your broker, and these fees would cut into your potential profits. If you are interested in stocks, you should look to mutual funds which, for a variety of reasons, are excellent investments for beginning investors.

More than two trillion dollars are now invested in some six thousand mutual funds. Over the past decade or so, more investors have put their money into mutual funds than in other investments. When you invest in a fund, you are buying shares in the fund. Your money is pooled with that of other investors, and the fund is run by a professional manager who decides what stock, government or private bonds, or other investments the fund should own. There are about twenty different categories representing the particular investment objective of the funds. Broadly defined, funds invest in stocks, bonds, or a combination of the two. Fund categories include:

Bond funds   These funds can invest in either private (corporate) or government bonds, such as municipal bonds.

Growth funds   These generally invest in stocks of well-known established companies.

Aggressive growth funds   These funds look for undervalued companies or companies that have fallen out of favor. These funds are best for long-term investors.

Sector funds   These are funds that invest in one industry, such as chemical or technology stocks.

Balanced funds   These funds hold a mix of common and preferred stocks and bonds and are more appropriate for conservative investors who will accept a lower return in exchange for less risk.

International funds   These funds hold stocks in overseas companies. They are extremely volatile because of their exposure to economic factors as well as currency fluctuations.

Income funds These funds invest in companies that issue dividends.

Usually, you will be required to make an initial investment of $1,000, but these minimum requirements will be waived in certain situations. For example, if the funds are used as a custodial account for your children or as an individual retirement account (IRA), you can usually open an account for $250 and sometimes less. Other funds will waive the minimum initial investment if you agree to have a regular sum, usually at least $50, deducted from your bank account and invested directly into the mutual fund.

The primary advantage to mutual funds is the benefit you get from the diversification of a fund's holdings. Funds own anywhere from a handful to hundreds of different stocks. While one or more stocks held by the fund may go down at a particular time, these losses will be offset by gains from other stocks held by the fund. Assuming you only had a relatively small amount of money to invest, you would not be able to get this much diversification if you bought individual stocks. Remember, though, like stocks, mutual funds are not risk-free. Stock funds did decline by some 20 percent during the 1987 crash, but overall mutual funds are excellent investments for individual investors.

Information on mutual funds and their performance can be found in the financial pages of newspapers and magazines. Financial publications such as *Business Week, Forbes,* and *Individual Investor* regularly survey the mutual fund industry. When you're evaluating funds, you should look for several funds that match your needs. Then, to narrow down your choices, see how the funds have performed over the past three to five years. Obviously, just because a fund performed well in the past doesn't mean it will continue to perform well, but if you're interested in a fund that has not performed well in the past, you should look for reasons why its performance is likely to improve.

A family of funds is a mutual fund company with many different types of funds. There are several reasons to invest with one fund family. Usually, it is easy to switch from one fund to another in the family. Also, you will receive one statement with details of all your fund holdings. Fund families generally offer you toll-free telephone access to your account information, check writing privileges, IRA accounts, etc. Because of the increasing competition among fund families, it's worth your time to compare how the services of one family stack up next to another family. Look first for a family of funds with several large funds that have been around for five or more years and have a good performance record. Make certain that the funds in your family match your investment needs. Then compare the extra services, such as phone privileges, free checks, newsletters, etc. Although it's unlikely you will find one family of funds that has the highest performing funds in all categories, you may want to keep your investments in one family because of the convenience. If you have difficulty reading account statements or hate keeping track of paperwork, then you may find it easier to stick with one family. Usually, all the funds in a fund family will have similar styles in paperwork and correspondence. Remember, though, the convenience of paperwork should not be the final reason you select a particular fund. There's no point sticking with a fund family unless you're confident in the performance of the individual funds as well as the service level of the company.

You can also use a discount brokerage to buy funds from different fund families. While you will be paying a commission, you will have access to a wide selection of funds, and the paperwork hassle is made easier by a single statement, which the brokerage will issue for your account. Charles Schwab and Fidelity both offer these services.

It's especially important that you compare fees. There has been a lot of publicity about no-load (no fee) funds that do, in fact, have fees for withdrawals. A true no-load fund is one that you buy directly from the mutual fund company without paying any commission. When you're comparing the return on funds, you must also compare fees. Obviously, any fees charged by the fund will cut into your profits. Here's a rundown on the various fees charged by most funds:

12b-1 fees   Funds charge from 0.25 percent to 1.25 percent of the assets to pay the marketing expenses.

Back-end (redemption) fees   Some funds charge you a percentage of your holdings as an exit fee when you sell your shares. Usually, back-end fees decrease the longer you hold onto the funds.

Management fees   These are fees, generally ranging from less than 1 percent to 2 percent of the fund's assets, charged to run the fund.

Reinvestment fees   These fees are a portion of your interest, dividends, and capital gains that are put back into the fund.

The prospectus of a fund will spell out all the fees; read this document carefully to make certain you understand all the fees. Remember, too, that if you buy mutual funds from a broker, you will also have to pay a brokerage commission ranging from 4 percent to 5 percent.

It's not necessary for you to own dozens of funds. For your first investment, you will probably feel most comfortable with a money market fund. However, once you have about $5,000 to invest and you have gained some confidence in your ability to choose funds, you will probably want to divide your money among three funds—a balanced fund, a growth fund, and a bond fund. If you're investing for the long term, such as for your retirement or for your kids' college tuition ten or more years in the future, you may want to follow a more aggressive strategy, putting more than half of your holdings in a stock fund and some holdings in an international fund. Because stocks outperform other investments, a common strategy is to subtract your age from 100 to estimate what portion of your portfolio should be in stocks. So, for example, if you're forty-five years old, you should have 55 percent of your portfolio in stocks (in mutual funds, this means equity funds—mutual funds that invest in stocks).

You may have heard the term "dollar cost averaging" in reference to mutual funds or other types of investments. This is simply a strategy designed to regularly increase your holdings in an investment. Dollar cost averaging works as follows: Every week or month, or at some other regular interval, you put aside the same amount of money to add to your holdings. For mutual funds, this means you will buy shares in the fund at whatever price they are at that moment. For example, if the net asset value of the shares is $5, your $100 investment will buy 20 shares; the next month, if the net asset value of the shares falls to $2.50, your $100 investment will buy 40 shares.

You will earn money on your funds holdings in several ways. Funds, like stocks, can pay dividends, which you can take as cash or reinvest in the fund. Some funds will provide capital gains when the fund sells some of its assets. Unless you need the money, it usually makes sense for you to add to your holdings and reinvest the dividends. Capital gains distributions are usually made near the end of the year. Before you buy a fund, find out when the distributions will be made. You could buy shares in the fund one day, get a capital gains distribution the next day and have to pay taxes on profits you didn't get. Remember, too, that even if you reinvest dividends, you will owe tax on the dividends.

What about the hot new fund that is getting lots of publicity? Remember, by the time you're reading about the fund, it may no longer be that hot. It is difficult to evaluate a new fund, because there is no past track record to review. But if you've done some homework and believe in the fund's strategy or are familiar with past funds run by the manager or the fund family, you may want to put a very small percentage of your holdings into the new fund.

Playing the Stock Market

Although mutual funds are almost always a better choice for small investors, you should still understand how the stock market works. Despite steep downturns in the market, such as the 1987 crash, stocks, over the long run, still dramatically outperform other investments. For the past seventy years, stocks have had an annual return of some 10.3 percent, nearly double the return on bonds and well above the inflation rate, according to Ibbotson Associates, a Chicago research and forecasting firm.

Not all companies issue stock; some firms remain private. By selling shares of stock, a company becomes public—meaning the shareholders (stockholders) own part of the company. You can buy common stock, which entitles you to voting rights, or preferred stock. Preferred stockholders do not have voting rights but would receive dividends before holders of common stock. As a stockholder, you will receive notices from the company on a quarterly and annual basis. You will be able to attend shareholder meetings, if you wish.

Why do companies sell stock? It is a way for corporations to raise money to expand, launch a new product, or otherwise expand the business. New firms that need money go public through initial public offerings (IPOs). Although IPOs do provide the chance to get in on the ground floor of a new company, they are also risky, since it's possible the stock will increase in value very slowly. You may prefer to buy stock in an established company.

Companies are listed—or traded—on one of several different stock exchanges. The oldest and largest is the New York Stock Exchange, which lists nearly two thousand different stocks. About eight hundred smaller and medium-size companies are listed on the American Stock

Exchange, and newer, less established companies trade on the NASDAQ (National Association of Securities Dealers Automated Quotation System).

The price of a stock (anywhere from a penny or higher) varies, according to how the particular industry has been performing, the overall economy, how analysts view the company's performance, and predictions of the company's earnings in the future. You will make money on your stocks in one or both of the following ways:

Dividends paid by the company When a company is performing well, it may choose to pay dividends to its shareholders. This means a certain dollar amount per share is paid to shareholders. For many years, people chose stocks such as those from well-established companies such as GE and IBM because of the regularly issued dividends.

Selling the shares at a profit Although you should view stocks as a long-term investment, you will want to sell if the price per share has risen substantially or if you think the stock has hit its earning peak. Hopefully, you will sell your shares at a higher price than what you paid for them. The difference between the price at which you bought them and the selling price, excluding any commission, will be your profit.

To help you decipher the stock tables in a newspaper, here are some basic definitions (reading across a stock table):

Hi/Lo (high and low) This indicates the highest dollar price and the lowest price the stock has had over the past year. A wide fluctuation means that you could lose a great deal or take large profits, depending on when you bought the stock.

Stock name and symbol This is the name of the company and its abbreviation.

Dividend per share This is the dollar amount you would receive for each share of stock you own if the company pays dividends. If company X pays a $1 dividend per share, and you hold one hundred shares, then you would receive $100 in dividend payments. Also listed is the dividend as a percentage of the current stock price.

Price/earnings (P/E) ratio This is the stock price divided by the earnings of the company for the past four quarters. Generally, the higher the P/E ratio, the better the stock, because people are willing to pay a price higher than the current value of the stock.

Volume This indicates how many shares of stocks were traded the previous day. Multiply this number by 100 to get the total number of shares traded.

Net change This shows you whether the stock has risen or fallen in price from the previous day.

Obviously, you will have to do a little more research before you buy a stock. You can get information from a company's annual report, quarterly earnings estimates, research reports from a brokerage, as well as other articles in the press. Another useful source of company information is Value Line investment surveys, which are detailed reports on specific companies updated regularly. You can use these reports to compare one company in an industry with its competitors. Other data you should review:

Earnings per share Increasing earnings per share means the company is growing.

Book value This is the net worth of the company, which will vary by the amount of assets.

Stocks are usually sold in round lots of 100 shares; if you want to buy a lesser amount (an odd lot), you will pay more in commission. You can use either a full-service or a discount broker. The full-service broker usually provides some research material and often makes specific recommendations. According to a recent survey by Mercer Inc., the average full-service commission on a trade of 100 shares at $3 a share was $81.07. Discount brokerage fees for the same transaction range from $24 to $35. Be wary of brokers that advertise even lower fees. Hidden fees can easily boost the cost of your transaction.

If you're comfortable doing your own research to select which stocks you want to buy, then you should use a discount broker to execute your trades. You will cut your commission fees substantially. Some discount brokers, such as Charles Schwab & Company and Quick & Reilly, will provide some of the offerings (such as research reports) usually available at full-service brokers, for additional fees. Some discount brokerages also offer all-inclusive accounts that allow you to make a variety of investments and let you write checks against your holdings. Usually, you will need to maintain account balances of at least $5,000 in these accounts.

Whether you're looking for a full-service or a discount broker, ask friends for recommendations. Then talk to a broker to get a feel for his or her style and approach to investments. Don't hesitate to ask the broker about his or her qualifications and experience. Look for a brokerage that is a member of the Securities Investor Protection Corporation (SIPC)—this means you will have some protection if the brokerage goes bankrupt. Most brokers will require you to sign a new account agreement before your first transaction. Before signing this agreement, make certain you understand its terms, including how you will pay for your securities, whether the broker can make any decisions without consulting you, and what level or risk you're willing to take with your investments.

In addition, many firms ask that you sign a document that legally binds you to arbitrate any dispute you have with your broker. You are not legally required to sign such a document; if you do so, you will not be able to sue your broker in the event of a dispute in the future. And if you want to find out whether the brokerage firm or the individual broker has been disciplined or investigated, you can call the National Association of Securities Dealers (800-289-9999).

For general investment information, including several useful brochures such as *Invest Wisely* and *What Every Investor Should Know,* as well as how to file a complaint against a broker and other useful tips, call the Securities and Exchange Commission (800-732-0330). For its annual survey of discount brokers, contact the American Association of Individual Investors (625 North Michigan Ave., Chicago, IL 60611; $4).

Especially if you're not meeting a broker in person, you may find it difficult to assess whether you and the broker can have a good working relationship. To help you get more of a handle on a broker's fees and investment style, ask as many questions as you can before committing yourself to any investment. Regardless of whether you're speaking with a broker who has been recommended to you or one who is soliciting your business, ask the following questions:

- How long has the person been a broker? How long has the broker been with the present firm? If the broker has been with the brokerage for only a short period of time, ask why he or she left the previous employer.

- What types of stocks does the broker generally recommend? You could ask the broker to suggest several stocks, then you could do your own homework and see whether you would be interested in those companies.

- How much commission will the broker make from you? Does the firm offer special incentives, like bonuses or trips, if certain stocks are sold?

- Does the broker have monthly or year-end sales quotas? Most brokers will not admit that they have to meet certain sales quotas. But if a broker repeatedly tries to sell you certain stocks at the end of a month or urges you to invest more than you're comfortable with, then the broker may be trying to reach his or her sales quota.
- Will the firm provide you with research material?

No matter how comfortable you are with your broker, don't forget that it's your money. If your broker seems to be pushing a particular stock, ask the broker why the stock is right for your portfolio. It's also very important that you regularly review all your account statements and contact your broker immediately if you think an error has been made.

Another popular way to get into the stock market is through an investment club. If you think these clubs are for experienced or wealthy traders, think again. There are some 13,000 clubs around the country with about 300,000 members. The club members follow conservative approaches in buying the club's holdings; they look for companies with solid earnings growth whose P/E ratio is below the firm's average P/E ratio for the past five years. The strategy behind clubs is simple: you work together with other small investors who have similar goals. Generally, members share the homework involved in researching and picking stocks. For a fun and informative look at one of America's successful investment clubs, read *The Beardstown Ladies Commonsense Investment Guide* (Hyperion; 1995). For information on starting your own club, contact the National Association of Investors Corporation (810-583-6242), a nonprofit organization that promotes investment in individual stocks. You can join this organization for $35 a year; your membership includes a copy of the organization's investment manual, its monthly magazine, as well as the right to purchase stock through the club.

You can also buy stock through dividend reinvestment plans (DRIPs). Some corporations allow you to buy shares of stock directly from the company. Once you own at least one share of stock in these companies, you can then purchase additional shares from the company without using a broker. Some of the companies that offer DRIPs are Exxon and Texaco. For details on which companies offer DRIPs, contact the National Association of Investors Corporation or read the *DRIP Investor Newsletter* (Charles Carlson, editor; 7412 Calumet Ave., Hammond, IN 46324; 219-931-6480).

Bonds

Bonds are another investment option. When you buy a bond, you loan money to the issuer of the bond. Bonds are issued by agencies of the federal government, local municipalities, and private corporations. You can purchase bonds individually through brokers or invest in mutual funds that hold bonds. The key appeal to bonds is that they regularly pay interest, usually every six months. In the past, bonds were generally viewed as an investment to be held for an extended period of time. However, the bond market has changed over the past few years and is more complex because of the greater variety in types of bonds and the increased fluctuation in interest rates.

Here's a simple way to understand how bonds change in value: When interest rates rise, bonds lose their value; conversely, when interest rates drop, bonds are worth more. Without getting into the rather complicated reasons why, you should know that when you buy a bond and interest rates rise, your bond is worth less and if you sell it, you would lose money. If you're not comfortable with this volatility of bonds, then you should only keep a small percentage of your holdings in bonds. You can also reduce your risk by holding bond mutual funds which, because of the many bonds in the fund, will allow you to ride out some of the interest rate swings.

When you're buying bonds, look for bonds that are rated AAA or higher by independent rating services such as Moody's. You can purchase bonds for amounts from $1,000 to $10,000 for different maturities—short term, intermediate term, or long term. Generally, the longer the term of the bond, the higher the interest rate offered, because your money is tied up for a longer period of time. However, returns on bonds are lower than returns on stocks over the long term. Another reason to consider bonds as part of your investment portfolio is as a tax shelter. Many bonds issued by local and state governments are tax-free; for example, if you live in New York and buy New York State bonds, you don't have to pay state tax on these bonds.

Annuities

Another investment option that has gotten a lot of publicity lately is the annuity. There are many different varieties of annuities, and they are available through brokers, mutual funds, and insurance companies. They are intended for long-term investing, primarily for retirement purposes. Variable annuities, sold by insurance companies, are a particularly popular type. You purchase an annuity of a certain value—say $10,000—and tell the seller of the annuity how you would like your money invested. Then, usually when you reach age sixty-five, you would receive your money back in the form of payments. You don't have to pay tax on the annuity until you get out your money, and your initial investment is guaranteed.

The return on your investment will vary, depending on how profitable the annuity's investments have been over time. In addition, management fees on variable annuities tend to be high, and if you withdraw your money within a few years of buying the annuity, you will have to pay high fees. As an insurance product, this is probably not your best choice. Furthermore, annuities are best if you are in a high income bracket and have already fully funded other retirement options, such as your 401(k) and other pension plans.

There are other investments that you've probably heard about—from real estate to junk bonds to commodity future options. These are intricate investments best left to a professional; they aren't appropriate for most individual investors, unless you have substantial portfolios and can withstand the higher risks involved.

DON'T BE SO QUICK TO SELL YOUR INVESTMENTS

If you have selected stocks and mutual funds, your investment will suffer losses at certain times. However, by holding your investments for long periods of time, you will also benefit from market upturns.

You've waded through the many investment opportunities and have selected the investments that you feel are best for your needs. As you accumulate more money to put into the investments over the months, you've used the dollar cost averaging approach to make regular investments. All these are good and positive signs. Now, a year later, you're starting to wonder whether you should switch mutual funds or sell that stock. Perhaps you've been reading reports about the economy or concerns about a particular industry. What should you do? Remember, the best investment strategy is one for the long term. A year may seem like a long time, especially if your investment has diminished in value, but a year is not a long time for most investments. You should hold many of your stocks and mutual funds for at least three to five years. And, if you hold them even longer, your return will be greater.

Shareholders holding onto stocks for a minimum of twenty years beat the performance of bonds, cash, and inflation 98 percent of the time, according to Ibbotson Associates.

You should still review your portfolio regularly. Your investment needs may have changed. Among the reasons for altering your strategy and considering buying or selling some investments:

- Your investment goals have changed. If your family situation has changed because of a marriage, divorce, birth of a child, retirement, or medical problems, then you should consider revamping the mix of your portfolio.

- A change in the investment itself. If, for example, your mutual fund is one of the worst performers in its category, then you should consider shifting out of that fund. You would also want to consider moving out of a fund if its investment strategy has changed dramatically or if the fund manager has left and you're not satisfied with the new manager.

- You need to find tax shelters. If you realize that you have paid much more in taxes for the previous year than you expected, you should review your holdings. Look for investments that will enable you to reduce your tax liability, such as tax-free bonds.

Remember not to view your investments as completely separate from your other financial decisions. You have to have a firm grip on your assets and liabilities so that you know how much money you have to invest. Likewise, your goals will impact what proportion of investments to keep in short-term versus long-term investments. And, although you will read about your retirement accounts in chapter 9, don't forget to include your retirement savings and investments in your calculations as you figure out your investment strategy. For example, if your IRA or 401(k) holdings are in stock mutual funds, then your nonretirement investments should be in different types of funds to allow you to benefit from the principle of diversification.

YOUR MONEY AND YOUR FUTURE ARE TIED TO YOUR INVESTMENTS

Don't let anyone choose or manage your investments without your authorization. If you do let someone manage your investments, make sure you set limits and continue to monitor your portfolio.

The old line—you have to lose some money before you can make some—is not far from the truth. You will have to take on some risk if you want higher returns on your money. It's not always easy to accept this fact. But if you do your homework and select your investments carefully, your money will grow over time. And, that's the whole reason to invest—to have more tomorrow than you do today!

CHAPTER 4

HOME SWEET HOME

That good old American dream of owning your home is still part of our culture, in spite of trying economic realities. Unfortunately, the dream is now more expensive: the median price of a single family home in 1994 was $109,400; in 1970, it was $23,000.

Buying a home is likely to be the largest expense you will have over your lifetime (unless you're paying for college for your children). However, it's not just the amount of money that makes the decision to buy a home unsettling and, on occasion, simply overwhelming. The notion of owning your home comes laden with emotional and intellectual considerations, such as whether you prefer an urban or rural lifestyle, what type of house you prefer, whether to live near relatives, whether you will have children, whether you or your spouse are able and willing to work to pay for the house, and more.

Perhaps twenty years ago, home ownership was equated with security. It was a virtual guarantee that your home would double or triple in value in a few years. Then came the devastating decline in real estate prices of the 1980s and early 1990s. Mansions in the oil centers of Texas were taken over by banks; palatial homes in southern California remained on the market for years, and houses in suburbs in the Northeast were sold for a fraction of their asking price. Today, not only is there no guarantee that your home will appreciate over time, you're often lucky if you're able to find a buyer for your home when you move.

It's obvious, then, that you should think very long and hard before you take that big step and buy a home. Think about how much time you put into researching other purchases, such as a new car or a home computer. You would probably spend months visiting showrooms and debating which model is superior, and then you would find every imaginable article about that car or gadget to make absolutely certain you're making the right selection. On the other hand, the decision to buy a home is often made quickly, after you've seen one home that you fall in love with. Even attending a handful of open houses isn't enough preparation for the major step of buying your own home.

HOME OWNERSHIP: IS IT FOR YOU?

Assuming you're absolutely certain you want to buy a home, you should have someone help you figure out the finances of buying one as well as the ongoing costs. An accountant or planner can help you estimate the after-tax cost of owning your home compared to paying rent. A banker can guide you through the mortgage maze, so you know what you will ultimately pay for the house over time. However, you're the only one who can decide whether you really want and/or need to own a home. Whether you're single, married, a parent, retired, or an empty nester, you should first evaluate some of the following factors:

- Do you put down roots and stay in one community for a long time? If you have moved frequently in the past for work reasons or simply because you haven't found a place where you want to settle down, then buying a home is probably not the best decision. Similarly, if you anticipate changing jobs within two to three years, the costs of the mortgage and the uncertainty over whether you could easily sell your home without taking a loss make renting a better option.
- Are you capable of doing your own repairs and small fix-up jobs? While you don't have to be a Mr. or Ms. Home Improvement to own a home, it certainly helps. Whether you buy a newly built home or a stately Victorian mansion, there will always be more work than you anticipated. In fact, experts say that you should expect to spend up to 5 percent of the purchase price on repairs and improvements during the first three years you own your home. And, while you may not mind living with a leaky faucet or an unfinished basement, there's another reason for keeping a house in good working condition. An attractive home that has been well-maintained will have far greater appeal to potential buyers when you decide to sell the house.

Being a home owner can be stressful: You wake up late and have to rush out of the house to an important appointment. There's no hot water and your driveway is covered with snow. Or, you're expecting a house full of guests over a holiday weekend and your septic system backs up. Something always happens, even when you do your best to keep up with repairs and regular maintenance. Assuming you have the funds, you can, of course, keep a Yellow

Pages handy and call on experts to handle emergencies and fix whatever is broken. On the other hand, you may feel more comfortable living in an apartment or a condo or co-op where you don't have to be responsible for repairs or maintenance.

- What is your lifestyle? Are you a prudent spender or do you have trouble paying your bills at the end of the month? Do you have expensive tastes in clothing, restaurants, or vacations? Owning a home is likely to be far costlier than you assumed. While you may have budgeted for your mortgage payments, property taxes, and higher utility bills, other expenses are bound to crop up. The furniture from your old residence may not fit into your new home and you may end up doing more redecorating than you expected.

  You may find, too, that you have to put in more work and time at home. It's not uncommon for new home owners to spend weekends, evenings, and vacation time around the house. Initially, you may not mind sitting in front of that fireplace you dreamed about for years. But, if you're used to frequently eating at four-star restaurants or taking extravagant vacations, then you may not want to buy a home—now or in the future. If you think you want a home but aren't ready to change your spending or saving habits, then you should postpone the decision until you do enough traveling to satisfy your wanderlust or have consumed so many rich meals that the local diner becomes appealing, and you're ready to settle down and become a home owner.

- Can you afford to buy a house? The real question may be whether you can afford to buy your dream home. Remember, though, unless you find a real bargain fixer-upper or a house at auction (probably a foreclosure that someone else could no longer afford), you must be prepared to make a major financial undertaking. In most cases, you will have to make a 20 percent down payment, or $40,000, on a $200,000 home. In addition to the down payment, you will have to pay other expenses related to the purchase, such as attorney's fees, application charges, insurance, inspection, title search, and more, which will total about 5 percent of the purchase price, or another $10,000. Different formulas are often used to assess how much you can afford to pay for your home, but a good rule of thumb is that you shouldn't spend more than 25 percent of your income on mortgage, house insurance, and taxes. Spending much more could leave you strapped and hard-pressed to pay all your other bills each month. Of course, you should already have from six months' to one year's worth of salary as emergency savings before you buy a house, in case you or your spouse gets sick or stops working.

- Is your income secure? Mortgage lenders look at how much you earn and your employment history to determine whether you're a good credit risk. You may qualify for a mortgage if you have a clean credit history and you've worked steadily, but you should also think about whether your job is stable. If, for example, you know that your employer is restructuring and there's a good chance that you'll lose your job, you should probably hold off buying a house. Also, if you work in an industry that has been downsizing, you should think long and hard about whether you would be able to keep up the mortgage payments if you lost your job. Likewise, if you're a freelance writer or a performer whose income fluctuates greatly—even if you qualify for a mortgage—you may want to wait until your income becomes more predictable before buying a home.

- Do you view your home as an investment? It's only natural to assume that the biggest purchase you'll ever make will increase in value over time. However, with real estate values fluctuating dramatically, you can't assume that you'll make a sizable profit when you sell your house.

  You should buy a home because you want a home, not because you're hoping to sell it for $100,000 more than you paid for it. Of course, you should try to buy a home in a stable community where house prices have been on the rise.

  You should do some research into the communities where you're looking. Find out whether homes have been selling for more or less than the asking price and what the average time on the market has been over the past few months. Check with the chamber of commerce to see if new employers have moved into the community. This information will give you a sense of the stability of a particular community. Still, you should not expect to make substantial profits from selling your home. You can assume that any profits you make will probably match inflation, roughly 3 percent in mid-1995, rather than provide you with double-digit returns.

- Are the tax breaks you'd get as a home owner important? Home owners receive significant deductions from the IRS; how valuable these deductions are depends on your income and tax bracket. Interest on home loans is deductible up to $1 million. This is one of the few substantial tax breaks available and one of the key advantages of home ownership. Also, when you sell your home and buy another at a price at least as much as the selling price of the first, you don't have to pay taxes on the profits (see the "Tax Tips" section at the end of this chapter).

WHERE TO MOVE

Okay, if you've carefully weighed all these factors and are certain that you want to buy a home, terrific! You've made a hard decision, and now you can begin to tackle the many nonfinancial issues. Can you live anywhere or are you limited to one or two communities because of family obligations or your job? Do you have young children who will be attending nearby public schools? Are you interested in a big city or a small town? While a real estate agent can supply you with basic data about an area, such as the number and size of the schools as well as the variety of recreational facilities, you should not simply rely on what the broker says, since he or she has a vested interest in your decision.

You should do your own firsthand investigations. If you're moving to a new city where you don't know anyone, it's especially important to make several visits to that area. One way to familiarize yourself with another region is to read the local newspaper. See if you can subscribe to weekend editions or read the publication at a library. When you do visit an area you're thinking about moving to, spend some time exploring on your own after the broker gives you a tour. You should drive as well as walk around the town to get a sense of the community. If you'll be commuting to work, make sure you drive during morning and evening rush hours to find out how long the trip is.

You should also explore a neighborhood at different times of the day. Notice whether residents use the parks or stores during the day. If you or your spouse will be staying at home with your children, you'll probably want to find an area where some neighbors are also home with children so that you don't feel isolated. If you have small children, see what activities are offered at schools or community centers. Go to the local school board office and find out whether the schools offer special programs, including classes for the gifted or afternoon activities, how large the classes are, etc. Check with local police to get the crime statistics for the neighborhood.

If you're trying to decide between several communities, it's a good idea to compare the cost of living in these communities. For a worksheet that compares specific issues such as state and local taxes, commuting costs, property taxes, and more, contact Right Choice (800-872-2294). For $190, this company will prepare a detailed cost comparison between your present residence and one other city.

COMPARING HOUSES

You can try and find your dream house on your own by reading the classified ads. But, in all likelihood, you'll want to use a broker, especially if you're moving to another city. Remember, though, no matter how friendly the broker is, the broker's commission is paid by the seller of the house. Your broker will certainly help you negotiate with the seller, but the broker is obligated to share all information with the seller. If you tell your broker the maximum amount you intend to pay for a home, the broker will relay this fact to the seller. You may want to consider using a "buyer's broker." This means that you hire a broker who acts on your behalf rather than that of the seller.

If you're looking for a home near your current residence, ask friends to recommend brokers they have used. Another option is to call brokers from listings in the Yellow Pages or in newspaper advertisements. Look for brokers who are members of the National Association of Realtors who also can use the multiple listings service; these agents will have access to houses that are listed through other brokers as well.

When you're looking at houses, with a broker or on your own, you should devise a simple system to help you remember significant details about the various homes you see. After all, if you're seeing half a dozen houses each weekend afternoon, then by Thursday night, it's hard to remember which house had the extra half-bath or the new kitchen tile. One easy way is to take along an inexpensive disposable camera to take pictures of any house that interests you. Or, hold a clipboard with a blank checklist where you can mark off details, such as the asking price, type of home, number of bedrooms, number of bathrooms, size of rooms, types of appliances, etc.

The Auction Option

If your budget is especially tight or you think that it will be difficult for you to get financing, you should consider buying houses sold at auction. These days, it's not just foreclosed homes in disrepair that are available at auctions. On occasion, new homes are auctioned off when a developer runs out of money and cannot complete the project. Check your local newspaper for auctions held by government agencies, banks, or construction companies.

You must still do the same homework for a house sold at auction as you would if you were buying a home from a broker. Find out the value of houses in the area and what comparable homes have sold for recently. Even if the house is brand new and no one has lived there, you should still have it inspected. Find out ahead of time what type of auction it is. Sometimes, the house will be sold to the highest bidder, regardless of the price. Other times, a minimum bid may be established, or the seller has forty-eight hours in which to decide whether to accept the highest bid.

In either case, once your bid is accepted, you will have to make a deposit of 5 percent to 10 percent of the suggested opening bid. Then you will have another month or so to pay the rest of the down payment. Unless you're comfortable with legal jargon, you should consult an attorney to make sure you understand the contract and whether you're able to back out of the deal. Also, you may want to approach a bank prior to going to the auction and start work on your mortgage application so you don't waste time. You may have to get your mortgage within a specified time period.

FROM OFFER TO CLOSING

Either you've had your own experience buying a home or you've heard horror stories from friends about all the hassles they encountered when they bought their first house. Unfortunately, most of the awful incidents are true. With so many details to be handled by both the buyer and seller, house buying (and selling) rarely proceeds smoothly. To give you a sense of the purchase process, here's a rundown of what to do once you find the home you want to buy:

1. Make an offer for the house, either directly, through your broker, or through an attorney.
2. Have the house inspected.
3. Apply for a mortgage.
4. Get your mortgage commitment.
5. Set up a closing date, when you will take title.

When you make an offer on the house, you will have to give the seller a binder, usually from $100 to $500, depending on the selling price. This money is placed in an escrow account and is returned to you if you decide not to buy the house. If you go to contract, the binder is put toward your down payment. You and the seller should sign a binder agreement that is in effect for about two weeks (long enough for you to have the house inspected) which should also state that you and the seller must go to contract by a certain date.

Usually, you will have to make a down payment of 20 percent of the purchase price. In the past, your down payment would be returned if the deal fell through. However, because of the pressure to sell in tight markets, today's contracts may spell out conditions under which the seller can keep all or a portion of your down payment. Some contracts specify that if the seller keeps the down payment, he or she cannot sue the buyer for breach of contract. In other cases, the seller can still sue for damages if the buyer backs out of the deal.

The conditions that let you get out of the contract are clearly indicated. These conditions include an unsatisfactory inspection; your inability to get financing; or the discovery of something drastic such as a lien against the property or that a crime was committed in the house. However, it's in the seller's interest to make it as difficult as possible for the buyer to back out, so you should urge your attorney to build in as much protection for you as possible.

The contract will specify the purchase price, but you may still be able to haggle even if you have agreed on a price. For example, if an inspection uncovers major damage, you could ask the seller to lower the price instead of simply paying for the repairs. This would be advantageous if you are planning extensive renovation and would prefer your own contractor to handle the work.

The contract usually stipulates: ". . . unless the inspection uncovers major structural damage . . ." Some contracts go farther and hold the seller responsible for repairs up to a certain dollar figure. In this case, assume that the inspection uncovers a leaky roof. The seller would have to pay for $7,500 worth of roof repairs, but you would be responsible for any bills that exceed $7,500 or whatever amount is specified in your contract.

Inspection

Never take either the seller's or the broker's word about the condition of the house. While some agents may recommend an inspector, you can also look for one yourself. Find an inspector who belongs to the American Society of Home Inspectors; membership in this group means the inspector has done more than 200 inspections. Expect to pay from $150 to $500, depending on the size of the house and where you live. The inspection should cover the following areas:

Temperature   Is the house adequately heated and does the air conditioning work properly? Is there enough air in all rooms, from attic to basement?

Plumbing   Are there any leaks in the basement, kitchen, bathrooms? Is there sufficient water pressure? Are all faucets and toilets working?

Wiring   Does the electrical system meet all codes and is it in working order? Are the electrical wires properly installed and grounded? Is the fuse box clean and are all the fuses working?

Foundation   Are there any water stains or other signs of structural damage in the basement?

Structure   Is any part of the house structure—walls, floors, roof, doors, attic, etc.—damaged?

Environment   Is there asbestos, radon, or other hazards in the house or on the property?

Insects   Some inspectors will look for termites, but if they don't, you should have the house inspected by a specialist.

In addition to providing you with a reason to pull out of the deal if the inspection uncovers something, contracts usually include a mortgage contingency that allows you to back out if you don't qualify for a mortgage. Rather than lose time and have to try to sell the house again if the buyer doesn't get a mortgage, some sellers have gotten tougher and have asked that the binder agreement or contract specify that the buyer will get a letter of approval from a bank within a week or ten days. Banks will usually issue this letter to prospective buyers who are likely to qualify for a mortgage. If you can't get this letter, then the seller is free to reshow his house and accept an offer from another buyer.

Appraisal

Another scenario that may or may not be covered in the contract involves the appraisal. In order to determine how much mortgage to grant you, lenders have the home appraised. Ideally, you want the appraisal to be close to the purchase price. If the appraised value is less than the purchase price, then the bank will extend a smaller mortgage. This means you may not have enough money to buy the house. Assuming the difference between the appraisal and the price isn't substantial and you're still interested in the house, you should approach the seller and see if he or she will help you finance the additional money. The seller may be willing to lower the asking price if he or she is eager to unload the house. On the other hand, the seller may decide to see if other buyers will meet the price in spite of the lower appraisal.

THE MORTGAGE MAZE

Like most Americans, you will need financing to buy your dream house. There are various options, such as taking a mortgage out from your bank or credit union, borrowing from relatives, or possibly even getting a loan from the seller. You should, in fact, start doing your mortgage shopping even before you find a house. While mortgage departments don't have the backlog of applications they did when interest rates were much lower, the mortgage application and approval process can still be lengthy. The earlier you start shopping for a mortgage and then complete an application, the less likely you'll have problems when you're trying to schedule a closing.

Your first inclination may be to apply only at banks where you already have accounts. However, you shouldn't stop there. Check with your employer to see whether it has any special arrangements with local financial institutions. If you're moving because you're being transferred by your employer, the company may be able to help you get a mortgage. You should also check with your credit union. In addition to visiting banks in your area, you can easily get information on mortgages from other lending institutions around the country. For $20, you can get a survey of mortgages from twenty to sixty banks in a particular area from HSH Associates (1200 Rt. 23, Butler, NJ 07405; 800-873-2837). On the other hand, if you have a troubled credit history and expect to have problems being approved for a mortgage, then you may want to consult a mortgage broker. Check with the local Better Business Bureau or consumer affairs department to make certain you use a reputable broker.

Hopefully, you've chosen a house that you can afford. You've now learned how to do a budget and understand what you're spending money on each month (see chapter 1). Once you know what your other monthly obligations are, you can decide how much you can afford to pay for your mortgage. But it's not just what you feel you can afford. Most banks don't want you carrying more than 35 percent of your monthly income to pay all your debts. That's why it pays to reduce outstanding amounts on any loans before you apply for your mortgage. Usually, banks will allow a mortgage, insurance, and property taxes up to 28 percent of your monthly income, with the remaining 7 percent allotted to other debt. One exception is the Alternative Qualification Program available through the

Federal Home Loan Mortgage Corporation (Freddie Mac) for first-time home buyers. Under this program, factors such as your household cash flow are considered rather than just the amount of debt you carry.

Down Payment

Assume that you will have to make a 20 percent down payment, although occasionally some banks will give you a mortgage if you make a smaller down payment (in this case, you will most likely have to get private mortgage insurance). Under some federal government mortgage programs, you may be able to put down as little as 5 percent.

If you have a savings plan in place well before you find the house you want to buy, you should have the money for the down payment. If you're determined to buy a house in the near future, then you should consider postponing that vacation or new car in order to have the money available for a down payment. If you need help making the down payment, you can ask family members to loan you the money. Anyone can give a gift of up to $10,000 to another person tax-free. If you can get the money several months or longer before you expect to buy the house, do so. That way, you can invest it and earn some profits, which, when added to your assets, will make you more creditworthy when you apply for a mortgage.

Fixed vs. Variable Mortgages

There are two basic types of mortgages: fixed and variable (also known as adjustable, or ARM), or some combination of the two, with the usual term of the loan either fifteen or thirty years. With fixed mortgages, you pay the same rate (averaging 8.49 percent for a thirty-year fixed and 8.04 percent for a fifteen-year fixed in the spring of 1995) for the life of the mortgage. With an ARM, the mortgage rate rises and falls with other interest rates. Slightly more than half of all mortgages taken out today are variable rates. ARMs are quite appealing, because their initial interest rates run about 2 percent lower than fixed rates. You should look for ARMs with interest rates that will not increase more than 2 percent a year or six points over the full term of the loan.

A hybrid, or convertible, mortgage may be a good deal if you don't expect to be in the house for the entire term of the mortgage. You would pay a fixed rate for a set period of time, often ten years, and then pay an adjustable rate. However, when the rate is adjusted, it can jump as much as 5 percent, which would dramatically increase your monthly payments. But if you're reasonably certain that you'll be selling the house before the adjustment, these mortgages can save you a lot of money.

When you compare mortgages, it's also important that you think about your lifestyle—including having children and whether you'll stop working—now and several years into the future. Meeting monthly payments may be a cinch now, when both you and your spouse are working. However, if you're planning to have children, you should do some calculations based on one salary or perhaps one and a half times your current income. Would you still be able to afford the same house?

If you're taking a variable-rate mortgage, it's very important that you assess your earning potential for the future. With this type of mortgage, your monthly payments can sharply increase when the rate is adjusted—within six months, one year, three years, or longer, depending on the type of variable-rate mortgage. If your income doesn't increase, will you be able to handle a monthly payment that is $100 or $200 more than your current mortgage obligation?

Interest Rates

Once you have a mortgage, you can't skip a month, the way you might with a credit card bill. If you miss making even one or two mortgage payments, you could lose your home. Be very clear how much you can afford to pay each month and do some careful comparison-shopping. Even one percentage point of interest makes an enormous difference when you consider that you will be paying your mortgage for fifteen or more years. If you want to get a sense of what you will be paying each month and over time, talk to a local banker who can give you a chart indicating different payments depending on interest rates. For example, according to HSH Associates, which tracks mortgage rates around the country, if you take out a $100,000 mortgage at 8.5 percent for thirty years, your monthly payment of principal and interest would be $769. If you sold your home and moved after seven years, you would have paid $57,668 in interest and would still owe $93,079. On the other hand, if you had a fifteen-year fixed-rate mortgage at 8.0 percent, your monthly payment would be $956, but after seven years, you would have paid only $47,876 in interest and you would owe $67,601.

The greater the down payment you make, the smaller the mortgage you will need to take. Obviously, you would then pay less in interest. However, if you think that your salary will increase substantially in a few years, you may opt for a lower monthly payment now rather than struggling to meet that higher monthly mortgage cost.

Other Mortgage Considerations

In addition to comparing interest rates and other terms of the mortgage, you should also consider other fees such as closing costs. To woo customers, some lenders offer free closing costs and may waive other charges depending on the size of your mortgage and your credit history. Listen carefully to what the bank charges for points—a fee of from one to four points can be charged on your mortgage. These points are deductible; you should know that on a thirty-year fixed, one point is equal to roughly .08 percent.

Necessary Documents

While your attorney handles the negotiation and writing of the contract as well as researching title questions and others, it's up to you to provide the bank with all the documents related to your mortgage application, such as employment history, tax returns, etc. You should double-check with your attorney or broker to make sure that you have all paperwork completed by the closing date.

Don't forget that you will need several certified checks; find out ahead of time so that you can have the checks drawn up (don't laugh; many a closing has been held up while someone frantically raced to a bank in order to get another check). Also, if you and your spouse or another person are buying the house, all of you must be present at the closing in order to sign the various documents.

It's inevitable that some hassles will happen right before and at the closing. Among the more common problems:

- Promised repairs have not been completed. For example, when you conduct your walk-through (your inspection of the house) a day before closing, you notice that the roof is still leaking. Rather than postponing the closing, you should ask the seller to deposit money in an escrow account. This money can then be used to pay for the repairs, which are listed in the contract.

- The buyer or seller needs to occupy the house either before or after the closing. You may need to get into the house you're buying early. Perhaps your contractor must start work so that you can move in by a certain date. If you and the seller have cordial relations and the seller has already moved out, you could try to negotiate a fee that will allow you or the workers into the house.

A similar situation could occur when the seller needs to stay in the house after the closing, because the house he or she is moving to isn't ready. Again, you could offer a rental agreement for a short period of time. However, some brokers say these situations can get messy—if, for example, the seller refuses to leave—and advise charging such a high rental fee that it will be easier and cheaper for the seller to move into a hotel. The best solution is to have a backup plan in case of emergency, for instance, you could stay with friends or relatives.

- Furniture that was supposed to stay in the house has been removed. The contract should include a detailed list and description of all the furniture and incidental items that are included in the sale. Sometimes, though, the seller will take these items, deliberately or by accident. When you conduct your walk-through and find that something is missing, immediately alert your attorney. If the seller refuses to return the item and you don't want to postpone the closing, you and your attorney will have to do some fast thinking to reach an agreement. Some brokers have even picked up the cost of some items themselves to keep a sale alive. Keep in mind, though, the relative price and value of the missing item. If you're buying a $250,000 house, is it really worth arguing over a $50 rug?

SELLING YOUR HOUSE

It's time to move up and out. When you decide to sell your house, you can use a broker and pay a commission of from

5 percent to 7 percent of the selling price. To find a broker, ask friends for recommendations or look at newspaper ads. Schedule appointments in your house with three brokers; you should not be charged for the visit.

Working with a Broker

Brokers may offer comments during their visit but, more importantly, they should follow up with a written plan spelling out what they would do to sell the house. Details about where the broker would advertise your house and whether he or she would hold open houses will be in this document.

Once you have selected a broker, you will probably be asked to sign an "exclusive" contract. This means that the broker will receive a commission even if you end up finding the buyer. If the broker insists on exclusivity, agree only for a specific period of no more than three months. If you don't have a buyer by then, you may want to rethink using that broker.

You and your broker will agree on the asking price. You can do your own checking by finding out the asking prices on similar homes in the area. You can look at newspaper listings or go to open houses yourself to find out the prices.

While most buyers will still have their own inspection, you may want to do your own. That way, you'll know whether there are any major structural or other problems such as a leaky roof, termites, etc. Depending on what it will cost to make these repairs, you may choose to do the work before you start to show the house.

Spruce It Up

You should also look at your house, both inside and outside, as if you were seeing it for the first time as a prospective buyer. This usually means you will end up making cosmetic and sometimes more substantial fix-ups. First, consider the outside entrance. Have your lawn freshly mowed and your garden well manicured. If buyers are coming at night, you will need to have a working light outside your door. Your front door should be freshly painted and the sides should not be chipped. Then, walk through each room. You want the rooms clean and uncluttered so that would-be buyers can visualize the rooms with their furniture in them. Keeping the rooms clean can be a problem, particularly if you have a large family with children and pets underfoot. You may want to put furniture in storage or place other items in boxes in your garage. Likewise, while you may adore your fuchsia kitchen, most buyers would probably be put off by the color. If you have an unusual-color paint or wallpaper, consider repainting the walls a more neutral white or beige.

While you're showing your home, it's a good idea to use a cleaning service every week or ten days. You may think that your home is already clean, but a professional cleaning will further enhance your home's appeal. You want waxed floors, scrubbed walls, an immaculate bathroom, grease-free ovens, etc. People generally look closely at kitchens and bathrooms, so these are the rooms you should keep particularly clean.

For Sale by Owner

Using a broker to sell your home will save you time and aggravation. The broker can show your home while you're working and screen all those pesky calls about your house. On the other hand, if you have the time and would like to save the money you would otherwise pay a broker, you can try to sell your home yourself. Be prepared for some hard work. Decide on your asking price after you've visited other houses. Check out open houses and see what features seem to interest prospective buyers. Other steps to follow:

- Interest on loans for your primary or secondary residence is deductible up to $1 million.

- Have a professional "For Sale" sign drawn and place it prominently in front of your house so it is visible by passersby on foot and in cars.

- For sales of homes after May 7, 1997, you can exclude up to $250,000 of gain ($500,000 if you're married and filing a joint return). You can use this exclusion once every two years, provided you have lived in your home for at least two of five years before the sale. In certain circumstances—including medical reasons or change in employment—you are entitled to a partial exclusion even if you haven't met the two year requirement.

- Prepare a data sheet to answer the most common inquiries, such as the utility charges, property taxes, name of school district, square footage, and any special features in the house.

- Have a sign-in book for anyone who comes to the house. That way, you'll know whether someone is returning for a second look.

- If you expect a big crowd, ask a friend or relative to help you, perhaps staying upstairs in the bedrooms while you're downstairs showing people the kitchen.

Finally, a word of caution: Don't try to deceive a buyer. Courts have sided with would-be buyers who want to back out of a deal when they find out some significant detail about your home. So, for instance, if someone has died in the house, you should tell a broker or prospective buyer. If there are specific problems such as radon, asbestos, or electrical-type problems, make repairs and have written receipts ready to show a buyer.

TAX TIPS

Owning a home is still one of the best ways to take advantage of IRS benefits. Among the basic rules:

- You can deduct all of the interest payments on your mortgage up to $100,000.

- If you sell your home, you don't have to pay taxes on any profits if you buy another home, costing as much or more than the sales price of your first home, within twenty-four months.

- If you are age fifty-five or older, you can permanently exclude $125,000 from the sale of a home whether or not you buy another house. To qualify, you must have lived in your home for at least three of the five years prior to the sale. Furthermore, you—or you and your spouse—only get this break once, so if you sell your home for far less than $125,000, you may want to take the exclusion at some point in the future. Also, if you're married for the second time and if either you or your spouse has already taken the exclusion in a previous marriage, you cannot take it again.

- Points—the up-front fees paid with your mortgage— are fully deductible in the year in which you pay them provided you buy, build, or remodel a full-time residence. The mortgage must be secured by your home and the points must be a specific percentage of the loan, not a flat fee, and the points must not be excessive compared to other banks in the area. Even if the seller ends up paying the points, you can still deduct them as the buyer, according to recent IRS rulings.

CHAPTER 5

PROTECTING YOURSELF AND YOUR ASSETS

D
o your eyes start to glaze over when you hear the word "insurance"? That's not an uncommon reaction to this complex subject. In fact, half of Americans with property insurance don't read their policies, and 60 percent say they don't always understand them! But if you've suffered losses in any of the recent natural disasters, such as the hurricanes in Florida, the California earthquakes, or the floods in the Midwest, you very quickly discovered what your insurance covered.

What is insurance? You pay fees, known as premiums, to insurers to buy protection against certain losses. Without this protection, you would have to pay for the losses on your own. For example, let's say that two farmers in the Midwest both lose their farms because of floods. One farmer has no insurance, so he is responsible for the entire loss of crops, buildings, and his future profits. The neighboring farmer had flood coverage, so an insurer will pay to replace the crops and buildings that were destroyed and compensate for loss of income. Except in very drastic situations, insurers can pay for the losses because the insurers have built up their assets by investing the premiums of all the policyholders. Then, when a loss does occur, the company has the funds to cover it.

Insurance that protects against the destruction of your home or property is just one type of coverage. Other insurance coverage is equally important. You should have insurance coverage in the following categories:

- Automobile
- Home owner's
- Life
- Medical
- Disability

You could read a book, in fact several books, on each of these types of insurance. This chapter will not cover every detail of insurance coverage. Instead, you'll get a brief overview of the types of policies available. Then, you can review your existing coverage to see whether it's sufficient or, perhaps, too much coverage. Or, you'll realize that you should get coverage for areas in which you don't have policies.

Don't postpone these decisions. As much as you'd rather not think about the possibility that you will need insurance, procrastinating on this issue can be very damaging. It's too late to get coverage when you need to collect on it: You can't complain about your collision coverage after you've been in a car accident. And it's pointless to wish you had more extensive medical insurance after you end up in an emergency room. Insurance is an integral part of your finances. Remember, to get your finances on healthier footing, you prepared a budget and started a savings plan. Getting the appropriate insurance is another part of the prescription to financial well-being.

CHOOSE YOUR POLICIES WELL

Insurance policies can be confusing, and while it's tempting to rely on the advice of whoever is selling you a policy, you shouldn't do that. Whether you're using a broker that your family has used for years or you're buying coverage directly from an insurer, it's important that you understand exactly what coverage you're purchasing, what you will pay today and in the future, as well as all the benefits of the policy. Take the time you need to review each point in the policy. And, if you're fortunate enough to have insurance coverage through your employer, read your employee benefits handbook so you know how extensive your coverage is. Make sure you understand what your employer's policies cover before you buy new coverage, or you could end up paying for duplicate coverage.

There is a lot of data on insurance policies available from the insurers themselves, consumer groups, companies that rate the insurers, and industry organizations. You can call the Insurance Information Helpline (800-942-4242; weekdays from 8 A.M. to 8 P.M. eastern standard time) to ask questions about your coverage, to find out how to complain about an insurance problem, and to request pamphlets on how to choose policies and cut your premium costs.

Do your homework and comparison-shop before you settle on a policy. For virtually all types of insurance, discounts are available. Don't assume the agent will volunteer details about the discounts; you should always ask what discounts are given. You may qualify for a discount with items that you take for granted, such as having airbags in your car or smoke detectors in your home.

Evaluate Your Current Policies

Your first step is to sit down and make a list of all your policies—the individual ones that you have purchased plus any coverage you have through your employer. If you and your spouse both work, don't forget to include policies from both employers. Pay special attention to medical coverage available through your employers. Employers have recently started requiring workers to pay for some or all of their medical insurance. If you're paying for coverage through your employer, you shouldn't pay for coverage through your spouse's employer if it only duplicates your coverage.

Don't assume that more coverage is better than less. In most cases, there's no reason to be covered under your employer's health plan as well as your spouse's plan. Insurers have gotten stricter about the coordination of benefits. After you receive reimbursement for medical expenses under your carrier, you will usually not receive coverage for the same expenses from your secondary carrier.

Shopping Tips

Once you have evaluated your existing policies, you're ready to consider replacing them or getting new coverage. Here are some general caveats that apply to most types of insurance:

- Don't buy a policy that is endorsed by a celebrity and sold on television or through the mail. Well, never say never, but chances are you could find the same coverage for less money on your own.

- Always ask who the insurer is. You may purchase all your policies from the same agent and barely pay attention when you pay the premiums. Insurance companies do fail, so you should always find out who the insurer is and check whether the company has received good ratings from the ratings services. A. M. Best, Moody's Investor Services, Standard & Poor's Corporation, and Weiss Research are reliable ratings services. You can check their reports in most

public libraries; look for companies that are rated A
or higher, or with grades of very good and excellent.
You should also look for companies that have been
in business for several years and are licensed in
your state (call your state insurance department for
this information).

• Pay attention to premium dates. Payment notices
are usually sent out well ahead of the premium due
date so that you have time to make prompt payments. It's just foolish to let a policy lapse because
you forgot to mail in your premium. If you have
trouble keeping track of the premium due dates,
mark your calendar or make notes in your checkbook. For example, if you know that you have to
make semiannual payments on your life insurance
policy, put a sticker on your calendar in May and
November or whenever your payments are due.

You should also try to make payment in full. If
you make installment payments, you will actually
be paying more for the policy. The insurer charges
you for the paperwork of having to process installment payments.

• Don't take coverage just because it's offered. Credit
card companies frequently send you letters about
their affordable coverage for life, home owner's and
other policies. Usually, this coverage will duplicate
coverage you already have. Some employers have
begun offering workers the option to purchase a variety of policies including medical, life, and auto
through payroll deductions. Review these policies
carefully; they may not be right for your needs and
may be more expensive than coverage you could get
on your own.

• Comparison-shop. In some cases—if you have a
serious illness or have been involved in several car
accidents—you may have difficulty getting insurance

and therefore won't have the option of searching for the best rates. However, most of you will be able to choose from a range of policies and find sizable discounts by getting several quotes. Don't hesitate to do your own research if your agent seems unwilling or unable to find you several options.

• Update your insurance. You will have to get new policies or amend existing ones as your family situation changes. For example, if you buy or expand your home, you need to amend your home owner's policy. If you have a child, you need to make sure the baby is covered under your medical policy. If you no longer drive one of your cars or you sell your old mink coat, you no longer need coverage for these items.

Agents

You should know that not every agent sells all types of insurance. Generally, you deal with one agent for your health and life insurance and another agent for your property and casualty insurance. The latter would include auto and home owner's policies. There are three types of agents:

Exclusive agents   These agents work for one company and only sell that company's policies. These agents receive either salary or commission.

Independent agents   These are self-employed agents who usually work for two or more insurers. They are paid by commission.

Brokers   Brokers can sell coverage available through many insurers, and they generally handle all types of insurance.

You should deal with someone who provides good service and with whom you're comfortable. Don't assume that you will get better service from an agent or broker than from a company directly. Companies that sell directly to consumers often have lower rates than other insurers. The following sections offer a look at the different types of coverage.

AUTOMOBILE INSURANCE

Although deciphering an auto insurance policy may be difficult at first, these policies are actually rather straightforward once you know that each policy includes distinct categories of coverage. It is especially important to comparison-shop for auto coverage. Premium costs vary dramatically depending on your driving record, the type of car you own, where you live, and other factors such as your age and health. Auto coverage includes the following sections:

Collision damage This covers your car for damages caused by another car or object. This coverage is costly, so you should consider dropping it if your car is more than five years old or if the collision portion of your premium is more than 10 percent of the value of the car.

Comprehensive coverage This covers theft, fire, and damages caused by something other than another vehicle. This coverage will pay for a rental car if your car is stolen. As with collision coverage, the older your car, the less comprehensive coverage you need. You can also have a higher deductible—say $1,000— to reduce the cost of your comprehensive coverage.

Bodily injury liability This covers medical bills for your passengers or anyone else who is injured by your car, regardless of fault. Some states require that you have a minimum amount of insurance for bodily injury, but you shouldn't scrimp in this category. Generally, you should have coverage of 100/300, which means coverage of $100,000 per person up to a maximum of $300,000 per accident.

Property damage liability This covers damage to someone else's property or car caused by your car. This category is less expensive than bodily injury, but you should try to get $25,000 worth of coverage.

Uninsured motorist This covers your costs if you're involved in an accident with someone who doesn't have insurance or if you're involved in a hit-and-run accident.

Medical coverage This is coverage that will pay the costs of medical care for you, the driver, as well as passengers in your car, usually up to a period of one year from the accident. Even if you have your own medical coverage, you may want to and may be required to take this coverage for your passengers who may not have their own medical policies. This coverage will also pay funeral expenses.

Some states are considered "no fault" states. Generally, it means that you will have to collect from your own insurer even if you did not cause the accident, and in most cases, you will not be able to sue anyone to collect damages. Also, some states require you to hold a minimum amount of liability coverage. But you should check carefully, since the regulations still vary from state to state.

You should shop around and look for all available discounts. Discounts are widely available, and you can save from 5 percent to 15 percent off your premium. For example, you are eligible for discounts if you: complete a safe driving course; install antitheft devices in the car; are a nonsmoker; have other policies from the same insurer; haven't had an accident in several years; or drive less than

1,000 miles annually. Another strategy to reduce your premiums is to raise the deductibles on the collision and comprehensive portions of your coverage.

When a teenager gets a driver's license, it's important that he or she be insured. Although your premium will go up when you add another person to your policy, it is generally less costly to add your teenage driver to your policy than to have the teen get another policy. You can reduce this added cost: some insurers give discounts if your kids get high grades, and when the kids go away to college and aren't driving your car regularly, then your premium may be cut.

If you live in regions where auto rates are high, especially in some cities, you may want to consider the cost of insurance before you select a new car. If you buy a car model that is more likely to be stolen, then you will have to pay a higher premium. To get a list of average rates for different cars, write to the Highway Loss Data Institute for its "Injury and Collision Loss & Experience" chart (10005 North Glebe Road, Arlington, VA 22202).

A few added tips:

- If you have several cars, it generally pays to insure them with the same company.
- Don't pay for towing coverage if you belong to an auto club and already have this type of coverage.
- Policies are generally issued for one-year periods; if you're thinking of switching before your renewal, compare the savings on the new policy to what you have already paid for your existing policy.

HOME OWNER'S COVERAGE

Coming home to find that your house has been broken into or destroyed by fire is undoubtedly one of your worst nightmares. When you discover exactly what you've lost and how many items can't ever be replaced, insurance is probably the last thing on your mind. However, having a good home owner's policy is crucial whether you own your home or condominium, or rent an apartment.

As with auto insurance, your policy depends on a number of factors, including where you live, what your home is worth, how valuable your possessions are, and whether you live in an area subject to extreme weather such as floods or earthquakes.

The jargon used to describe home owner's policies is easy to understand. The coverage ranges from HO-1 to HO-8. Generally, most home owners have HO-3 coverage, which is extensive and affordable; HO-4 is coverage for renters, and HO-6 is coverage for condo owners. Remember, though, that the HO-3 policy will not cover damage caused by floods, earthquakes, and certain other extreme conditions. You will have to get a supplementary policy to protect against these disasters.

The most important part of your home owner's policy is the "replacement clause." This is the money you would receive to pay for the damages. You should insure your home for at least 80 percent of the replacement value— that is, what it would cost to rebuild your home. What you paid for your home may be far less than the replacement value, especially if you have lived there for several years or have renovated and expanded the house. Ask an experienced appraiser or broker in the area to estimate what it would cost to rebuild your home today.

Also, you should regularly review your policy to see if it needs to be updated. You will need to revise your coverage if you have made any improvements to your home or bought costly items such as computers or stereo equipment. Be aware, however, that most home owner's policies have limits to what valuable items are covered. If you have furs, expensive jewelry, computers, antiques, etc., you should get a valuables rider. You will have to submit a detailed description of the items and pay an added premium for this rider.

Another rider—generally costing less than $200 annually—gives you a one million dollar umbrella policy, which provides liability coverage beyond the limits of your home owner's and automobile policy. This coverage would kick in if, for instance, someone falls on your sidewalk and sues you for damages. Although you may not think you need this coverage, you'd be surprised how easily you can incur medical and legal expenses if someone is injured in your home.

If you work from your home, review your coverage carefully with an insurance agent who is familiar with business policies. Generally, most home owner's polices specifically exclude office equipment from the coverage. You would have to get additional coverage for any equipment as well as liability coverage for your employees and anyone else you meet with in your home office.

You won't be able to insure every last item in your home. It's crucial you insure your home itself for 80 percent of its replacement cost. On the other hand, it is probably too expensive to cover every last appliance and piece of furniture for 100 percent replacement cost. Discuss your options with the agent.

Discounts are also available on home owner's policies. Tell your insurer if you're a nonsmoker and have smoke detectors in your home.

If you live in an area that the government has labeled as a high risk for floods or earthquakes, you may qualify for special government insurance. Contact your state insurance department to find out whether you qualify for this insurance.

You should take photographs or a videotape of the exterior of your home as well as the contents. Do this every two years, or more often if you renovate your home. Keep the videotape or pictures in a safe deposit box or at a relative's house. That way, if your house is damaged and you want to collect on your policy, you will be able to show the insurer what your possessions and your home looked like intact.

What should you do if something happens and you have to collect on your policy? You should, of course, immediately contact your agent or broker. He or she may have specific instructions. You will also want to contact the police, in the event of theft, in order to file a detailed report of what has been stolen. If you can stay in your house, you should try to separate what has been damaged or else take pictures to show the insurer what has been damaged. If you have to move to a hotel or motel, keep copies of the bills and receipts for your meals, clothing purchases, etc.

Even if the insurer sends someone to inspect your home, you should write a detailed report to your insurer within sixty days of the incident spelling out exactly what was damaged or stolen. The insurer and adjusters will review your claim and either pay the amount you have requested or else a lesser or greater amount. If you're unhappy with the settlement offer, you should try to negotiate through your agent or directly with the insurer. If you are still dissatisfied, you should call the National Insurance Consumer Helpline (800-942-4242) or contact your state insurance department.

DISABILITY INSURANCE

Many of you assume that you have adequate disability coverage through your employer or that you will automatically receive Social Security if you become disabled. Unfortunately, you should not count on either type of coverage being enough to cover all your living expenses. Social Security benefits are paid to only a small percentage of the people who become disabled. And, while many employers do offer disability insurance, the coverage is usually not as broad as you assume it is. First of all, the coverage may be limited to disabilities caused directly by a job-related accident. Or the coverage may be limited to a relatively short period of time. Still, since it can be difficult and costly to get disability coverage on your own, you should take the coverage provided through your employer. Review the policy carefully. Make sure you understand how the policy defines disability. Does it mean that you cannot work at all, or that you are unable to perform at your previous job?

Disability insurance is intended to replace the salary that you would lose if you were unable to work. However, you cannot get coverage for your entire salary; if you could, you along with many other people might choose to stay on disability permanently. Most policies will replace roughly 60 percent to 70 percent of your salary. If you have coverage from your employer but feel that it is inadequate, see whether you can get supplemental coverage from the same insurer. If you don't have disability coverage through your employer, try and purchase it through another group such as a professional or trade organization.

Disability insurance works as follows: You pay a set annual premium to cover a disability. The cost of the premium will vary by several factors, including your age, sex, occupation, and whether the policy is adjusted for inflation. Other important clauses in the policy that you should review include:

The benefit period This details the length of time benefits will be paid.

The waiting period This details the number of days before you will begin to receive payments.

The maximum payment This is the most your policy will pay.

Noncancellable and guaranteed renewability You want this clause, or else the policy could be canceled at any time.

The length of payments   Payment periods can last from one year through the rest of your life. Generally, depending on your age at the time you get the policy, you should try to get coverage that will last until you turn sixty-five (you will then be eligible for Social Security).

Obviously, the more coverage provided in your policy, the higher the premiums will be. You will have to weigh the importance of having certain coverage compared to what you will pay for the policy. There are some strategies that will reduce the cost of your policy. If you lengthen the waiting period coverage to 90 or 120 days, your premium will be lower. Also, you may want to skip the inflation rider, since inflation has been fairly low these days.

Any money paid to you from an individual disability policy is not taxable. However, disability payments from an employer's policy are taxable.

MEDICAL COVERAGE

Recently the United States faced the prospect of a major health care reform that would have radically changed our medical system. Although it seems unlikely that a national health insurance system will be instituted in the near future, there have been some significant changes in medical coverage. Medical costs have been rising steadily, and both patients and doctors have felt the impact of these increases. Fewer employees—148 million in 1994 compared to 152 million four years earlier—receive medical coverage through their employers. And, if your coverage hasn't been reduced or eliminated, it's likely that you will be asked to pay some or all of the cost of the health insurance.

Some forty-one million Americans have no health insurance. This can be a serious problem, because a major accident or devastating illness could deplete your savings in a very short period of time if you have to pay all the bills on your own. There's no question that you need some type of health insurance. While you wish you could return to the old days when you visited your family physician, left the nurse an insurance form, and frequently didn't have to pay any charges, you'd better get used to medicine in the 1990s. Not only do you have to figure out how to pay your doctor bills up front, you will have to find doctors you have confidence in and coverage with premiums that won't wreck your budget.

Again, it's worth stressing that, although you may qualify for certain government programs and you should certainly investigate these programs, you shouldn't count on getting coverage under a federal program. Medicaid will cover medical costs for people whose income falls below certain levels. For those age sixty-five and older, Medicare will pay for some health expenses. Part A of Medicare provides for hospital and nursing home coverage; part B covers doctor and drug bills. For information on Medi-care, contact your local Social Security office or your state department on aging. These offices will usually also provide you with free coverage on medical insurance and how to evaluate policies.

There are three basic types of medical coverage available:

Traditional plan   This is the old system where you visit a doctor of your choice and either have the doctor submit a claim to your insurer or you pay the doctor directly and are reimbursed by your insurer. Usually, you have to meet an annual deductible, from $100 to $250, before your bills are covered. Also, benefits may be limited to certain dollar amounts.

Health maintenance organizations (HMOs) These are groups of doctors that have essentially formed corporations. The doctors can charge less for their services because of their arrangements with the insurers. When you join an HMO, you will generally pay a flat annual fee, which varies according to the arrangement your employer has negotiated with the HMO. Usually, you are allowed unlimited visits to the HMO and pay a modest fee such as $5 or $10 per visit. If you need to see a specialist, the HMO will refer you to one. If you don't have coverage from your employer, some HMOs will let you join as an individual. Although you often pay lower fees at an HMO than you would under traditional plans, you may not be comfortable with the arrangements available through the HMO. In most cases, you will not see the same physician for each visit. Usually, your employer will offer you a choice of HMOs. If you're considering using one, investigate their services before joining. Ask other patients about their experiences; ask how long they wait and how easily they're able to get referrals to specialists. Also check whether the doctors within the HMO are board-certified.

Preferred provider organizations (PPOs)   Coverage under these plans is similar to HMOs; usually, you only have to pay a modest copayment charge of $5 to $15 per visit. You select your primary care physician and certain specialists from a list of doctors who belong to the PPO. If you choose to see a doctor who is not part of the PPO, you will be reimbursed for some, but not all, of the doctor's fees. Usually, you will also have to meet a higher annual deductible if you see doctors outside of the PPO. As with HMOs, in order to see a specialist, you first have to get a referral from your primary care physician in the PPO.

Even if you're not completely satisfied with the coverage available through your employer, don't discard your medical coverage in haste. If you have to get a policy on your own, the premium costs may be prohibitive. Premiums for traditional coverage can run as high as $5,000 annually for an individual and $13,000 for a family of four. Joining an HMO can cost individuals $2,000, and coverage for a family of four can cost $6,000 per year.

When you review any medical coverage, you should make sure that visits to your doctor as well as hospital stays are covered. Ideally, you would like a hospital plan that pays 100 percent of your hospital costs for a set period of time, such as 120 days, and then 80 percent of additional costs up to a certain limit, after which it will pay all costs.

Remember, too, that if you leave your employer, a federal law, COBRA, gives you the right to continue your existing health coverage usually for up to eighteen months, provided you pay the cost of the insurance. To get this coverage, you must fill out forms available from your employer within sixty days of leaving your job.

Some additional pointers to keep in mind:

- If your coverage is ending, don't wait until the expiration date to apply for a new policy. For example, if your child is graduating from college or reaching age twenty-five and will no longer be covered under your plan, make sure he or she applies for new coverage.

- Look for one-year coverage that is guaranteed renewable.

- Look for an annual lifetime benefit limit of $250,000.

- Try and get the lowest copayments possible.

- Look for generous psychiatric, dental, and other special policies.

- Be truthful on your application. If you fail to mention certain conditions, the insurer could refuse to cover these illnesses in the future.

- Consider buying a supplemental long-term care policy. These can be costly but are important because of the often prohibitive costs of extended nursing home stays. Information on these policies is available from brokers, the American Association of Retired Persons (AARP), and other senior resource centers in your community. The premiums rise but cost less when you buy them at a younger age.

LIFE INSURANCE

This is probably the most important insurance that you'll need. After all, everyone should have life insurance, right? Well, life insurance is essential for most, but not for everyone. Life insurance is intended to replace your lost income and help your survivors pay for living expenses after your death. If you're young and single and no one is dependent on your income for his or her well-being, then you don't need insurance.

Wait a minute, you may be saying, isn't it prudent to buy insurance when you're younger, healthier, and the premiums are less? It's true that premiums tend to rise as you get older. However, if you don't need to have a policy, you could take the money you would otherwise use to pay premiums and invest it elsewhere. There are some types of life insurance that are essentially investment options, but you should consider these options very carefully, because there are often fees and charges that will cut into your investment returns.

How much coverage do you need? Experts disagree on how much coverage is necessary. If both you and your spouse work, your first priority should be to get insurance on the spouse who earns more. One rough rule of thumb is to buy coverage worth five times the higher salary of yourself or your spouse. If you have a child, you should have six times your salary; for two children, seven times your salary.

Another way to estimate how much coverage is necessary is to figure out how much annual income your family would lose if you died. Then, subtract any other income sources, such as savings, interest, dividends, and Social Security benefits. The amount left is the amount you will need to replace. You could then search for a policy that would pay this money for some specified period of time, presumably until your family could get back on its feet. If you think that you or your spouse would have to stop working if one of you passed away, don't forget to account for the loss of this salary.

There are two basic types of life insurance: term and cash value. Term is an older and traditional form of insurance that, until the last twenty years or so, virtually everyone bought. You pay annual premiums for a set period of time, usually from five to fifteen years. If you pass away during this period, your beneficiaries receive a death benefit, which is the face value of the policy. Term policies are popular, because they are far less expensive than other types of life insurance. Ask a broker to suggest several policies, or call companies directly to see what their policies will cost. Two reputable companies that sell direct are Ameritas Life (800-552-3553) and USAA (800-351-8000); the latter only handles people with some military affiliation.

One of the drawbacks to term policies are the increasing rates. If you buy a term policy when you're age thirty, you could get a $400,000 policy for about $500 a year (a whole life policy for the same person could cost three to four times as much). However, the premiums will rise each year and when you're middle-aged they can increase substantially. Before you purchase a term policy, ask how much the premiums are likely to increase over time and what you will pay for the entire term of the policy. You could also buy term insurance with level premiums. You pay a higher premium, but the premium remains the same for the life of the policy. Or you could simply shop around for a lower premium. There's no penalty if you drop a policy, so if you find a policy with a less expensive premium for the same amount of coverage, you could simply drop your existing policy and buy the new one.

Cash value—also known as whole life or universal—is the other type of life insurance available today. These policies are actually insurance combined with a tax-deferred savings plan. Some of your premiums become a cash reserve, which is invested by the insurance company. When you die, your beneficiaries will get the death benefit specified on the policy. On the other hand, if you decide to cash in the policy, you are entitled to get some of the cash reserve.

You can also borrow against your cash value policies; you will usually pay interest two to three points higher than the prime rate. Any money that you don't repay would be deducted from the death benefit. The three key variations on cash value policies are as follows:

Whole or straight life   You pay set premiums for the term of the policy. When you've paid all the premiums, the policy remains in effect until your death. You also accumulate a cash reserve, but the insurer decides how this money is invested.

Universal life   In this type of investment policy, you can vary the amount of your premium by using some of the cash reserve to pay it. You can also increase or decrease the amount of the death benefit. But you do pay administrative fees for this flexibility. The insurers invest your money in short-term bonds, and the return is usually set annually.

Variable life   These types of policies have gotten a lot of attention lately because of the many different investment options available through them. You can select the investment, and the value of your policy fluctuates according to how these investments are performing. However, the value of your policy will never fall below a certain minimum guaranteed amount.

Variable life policies are in fact considered securities, so you must buy them from a licensed registered brokerage salesperson. You will have to review the prospectus and weigh the risks, as you would with any investment opportunity. Obviously, these are riskier types of policies, and you may not be comfortable insuring yourself this way.

Without examining your particular needs, it's impossible to say whether term or cash value is a better option for your insurance needs. But if you're married and have children, and your choice is no insurance or term insurance, then you should definitely get the term coverage. Try to find an affordable term policy that gives you the option to switch to cash value in the future.

Two companies that will provide quotes on life insurance policies are SelectQuote (800-343-1985) and Quotesmith (800-556-9393). And if you want a policy evaluated by an objective third party, contact the nonprofit National Insurance Consumer Organization (NICO), which will evaluate policies for a fee of $40 for one policy and $30 for each additional policy (202-547-6426).

POLICIES YOU DON'T NEED

Insurance is available for every imaginable catastrophe, but it's unlikely you will need such protection. Don't buy a policy just because it's available. Avoid the following types of insurance, which are usually expensive and unnecessary.

Coverage for specific illnesses There are policies that cover you if you get cancer or lose a limb. You need comprehensive policies that cover you for all medical problems, not selected ones.

Accidental death policies These policies are frequently sold in airport kiosks and are designed to pay you a double or triple death benefit if you're killed in an accident. While the policies aren't expensive, it's not necessary to buy a policy designed to protect against an accident. You should buy life insurance that helps your survivors, regardless of how you die. Also, when you're traveling, your credit card company may make flight insurance available at no charge.

Contact lens loss You don't hear as much about these policies as you did in the past when contact lenses were more costly. But you don't need the insurance, especially if the premiums cost more than the lens.

Credit card insurance The cost of these hot line services isn't much—usually around $25 to $75 annually—but that's an expensive way to pay for convenience. When you lose a credit card, you are limited by law usually to the first $50 of unauthorized purchases, provided you notify the bank. The credit card hot line services will cancel your cards, but especially if you're also covered under your home owner's policy, there's no point in taking this coverage.

Credit/life/credit property insurance When you take out a mortgage or a loan, the bank will often offer you insurance that would pay off the loan. However, you don't have to take this insurance in order to get the loan. And if the cost of the insurance is added into your loan, you'll pay more over time for the loan. When you're reviewing your assets and buying life insurance, you should bear in mind the mortgage that your survivors will have to pay.

Insurance on your children New parents are often solicited by agents who urge the parents to buy life insurance for their babies. Although the policies may be inexpensive, there's no point to buying coverage on your kids . . . at least until they become child stars who are supporting the rest of the family!

CHAPTER 6

ONE BIG HAPPY FAMILY

I f you have children, you already know all too well how expensive it is to raise them. Even if other parents warned you, the expenses of the first year alone can be astounding—experts say it's not uncommon to spend an estimated $7,000 on your child from birth to his or her first birthday. That's a lot of diapers, formula, clothing, medicine, and assorted paraphernalia including car seats, swings, blocks, mobiles, etc. If you've ever spent any time in baby departments, you know how quickly and easily the dollars just disappear on behalf of your beloved offspring.

When your baby gets a little older, you'll have to pay a sizable monthly bill if you send your toddler to day care or nursery. Even more alarming is paying private school tuition for elementary school, which can cost from several hundred dollars to $10,000 depending on your choice of school and where you live. It's not surprising, then, that the U.S. government estimates it will cost well over $100,000 to raise a child to age eighteen. And that's a conservative estimate. If your child has special medical problems that aren't covered by insurance, the tab will go much higher.

However, some of these day-to-day expenses seem paltry compared to the cost of a college education. In addition to the concerns that all parents have about feeding, clothing, disciplining, etc., the biggest worry is undoubtedly saving for your child's education. Because of this pressing priority, most of this chapter will focus on how to formulate a college savings plan if you don't already have one and what to do if you need to save even more than you anticipated.

Some costs associated with raising a family have developed recently, in the last twenty or so years. The American family faces issues that many of our parents and grandparents never had to consider. Gone are the days when one parent, almost always the father, went to work and left the other parent home to raise the children. Today, nontraditional families headed by two-career couples and single parents are far more common, with everyone trying to juggle their schedules to accommodate each other. From a financial planning standpoint, in addition to needing more money to raise your children, you have many other concerns as well—child care, employer benefits, insurance, etc.

PRE-PREGNANCY PLANNING

Even if you're already on comfortable financial footing, as new parents you will have to reassess almost every aspect of your plan. The best time to address these issues is before you have children. In many cases, you and your spouse have planned for a family. Perhaps you've already bought a house or rented a larger apartment. Presumably, you already have a strong savings and investment plan in place. If you're still saving for a home, then you will have to revise your budget after the baby arrives, if not before.

You have to consider the loss of a salary, at least for a time after the baby is born. Find out what your employer's maternity policy is ahead of time, so you can make plans accordingly. If your employer has fifty or more workers and you have worked there for at least one year, you are protected by the Family and Medical Leave Act. Your job must be held for you while you take up to twelve weeks' leave, usually unpaid, after you have a child or adopt one. Check your company benefits office; some generous employers offer financial help if you're adopting a child.

You should also utilize other company plans, both as a way to save for the future and reduce your taxes. You should contribute the maximum allowed to your company's 401(k) plan. Not only does your money accumulate on a tax-deferred basis until you withdraw it, but with your company's matching contribution, you're essentially getting "free money."

Health Insurance

The first issue that you must deal with is health insurance. If neither you nor your spouse has insurance, you may find it difficult to get a policy that will cover a pregnancy. Many policies have a waiting period, but you should still look around for a policy, since you'll certainly want to have coverage for your child. If you don't have coverage, you will have to pay the cost of prenatal care and the delivery out of your savings. Normal deliveries average about $6,500; cesarean births will run several thousand dollars more.

If you have insurance, review your policy carefully so that you comply with any special requirements regarding pregnancy. If both you and your spouse have coverage, usually, you will have to decide under which policy to insure your child. You should compare policies to see whether standard checkups are covered, since your baby will have a dozen or more well visits during the first year. If you have the option of a traditional policy or an HMO, do your homework and make sure you're comfortable with the doctors that will be treating your baby. Finally, if you pay for coverage, either on your own or through an employer, make sure that you're not paying for duplicate coverage. If you are, try to consolidate the coverage and put that additional money into savings.

Find out whether your child is covered immediately at birth or when you have to send notification to your insurer. If you're adopting a child, make sure you tell your insurer, to avoid hassles at a later date.

Remember to take advantage of your flexible spending account (FSA) if your employer offers one. The plan works as follows: you are allowed to contribute up to $5,000 of pretax salary each year. You can then use the money to pay for child care costs or certain expenses that are not covered by your insurance—deductible payments, unreimbursed medical bills, medicine, glasses, etc. You'll have to estimate your expenses carefully, though, because any money that you don't use in the account is forfeited.

Protection for Your Family

If you haven't drawn up a will, make sure you do so after the birth of your child. It's important that you name a guardian to care for your child, in the event you and your spouse die. There's no doubt this is a difficult subject, but it is something you must deal with (for more advice on wills, see chapter 8).

Make sure you have sufficient life and disability insurance. Again, while you may have felt that you didn't need this coverage up to now, as a parent it's especially important that you protect your family against a catastrophe or your death.

CHILD CARE

It's easy to joke about the schedules of a two-income couple. The so-called yuppies of the 1980s have grown out of the dink (double income–no kids) stage into the frantic family stage. Everyone rushes around in the early morning to get dressed, grab lunchbags or briefcases, and depart for school, work, and other spots. But if you think that a busy schedule is offset by the extra income that two-income families have, you're probably wrong. Usually, only a relatively small portion of the second income is kept by a two-income family because of child care costs, transportation, and of course taxes.

Another side of the child care dilemma is evident in single parent households. Not only are finances likely to be quite tight in these families, the working parent has far less flexibility. If he or she has no helpful friends or family to provide back-up help, the single parent must arrange a compatible work and child care schedule.

Child care is both a financial burden and one of the most traumatic issues for parents. Unless you're fortunate enough to have a grandparent, sister, aunt, or other relative willing to provide free or low-cost child care, you have to figure out which option is best for you. Among your choices:

Child care in your home To avoid the Zoe Baird problem, you must be careful to comply with IRS regulations regarding hiring help. In 1993 President Clinton nominated Baird for the position of attorney general, but she withdrew from consideration after revealing she had not paid taxes for her domestic help. You may want to consult an accountant to make sure you fill out the appropriate forms and make all necessary payments.

You are required to pay Social Security and Medicaid taxes for your caretaker, assuming you pay this person more than $50 per quarter. In addition, you will have to withhold federal and, in some cases, state unemployment taxes. You may also withhold income taxes, depending on your caretaker's preference. For the exact rules on your responsibilities, contact the IRS and request Publication 926, *Employment Taxes for Household Employers,* and Publication 927, *Employment Taxes and Information Returns.* Or ask the IRS for a packet containing all the forms and information you need for household employees.

Day care center You can choose to leave your children at a day care center. Assuming the center is licensed, you may be able to get a child care credit or take advantage of an FSA account. The tax credit is a credit given to parents who work. The credit is a percentage ranging from 30 percent down to 20 percent of the first $2,400 that you spend on child care for one child or $4,800 for two or more children. Generally, if your income is over $24,000, it pays for you to take advantage of an FSA rather than the tax credit.

Au pair You can arrange through various agencies to hire either an American or a person from another country to live with your family and care for your children for periods of one to three years. Generally, when you hire a foreign au pair, you are responsible for paying health insurance and the cost of transportation to the U.S., which will usually set you back about $3,500.

COLLEGE SAVINGS

Hopefully, sending your children to college will be much less stressful than sending them off to day care when they were very young. However, while you may not have as big an emotional burden, you'll have a hefty financial one.

With college costs increasing by roughly 7 percent annually, it will cost some $270,000 to send your child (born in 1995) to four years at a private college. Even state universities, once considered a safe haven if you couldn't afford a private school, have become costly as well; four years at a state school will run you some $130,000.

Because of the high cost of higher education today, it's imperative that parents start their savings program as soon as possible. It makes more sense for parents to be ready to pay at least a portion of the college expenses, rather than waiting until the child is preparing to start college. Remember, though, that there are alternatives if you simply don't have the funds and your child doesn't qualify for financial aid. Your child could attend college part-time, or start out at a lower-cost community college and then transfer to a four-year institution. And, if you've diligently saved for college and your son or daughter chooses not to attend, those monies can certainly be used for other purposes such as your retirement or a new home.

The key to creating a successful savings plan for your child's education is to realize that you're not expected to, and don't have to, save four years' worth of tuition and fees. Remember, in addition to financial aid, there is a variety of funding available from colleges, federal and state agencies, and other private sources.

Especially if you have several children, trying to accumulate enough to pay for the entire cost of their college education is virtually impossible. If you focus on saving what seems an impossibly large sum, like $100,000, you may simply procrastinate and waste valuable time when even a small amount of savings could be compounding and growing. Or you may begin spending wildly as a way to drain their savings, assuming that if you can't save enough to pay for the tuition, you might as well have no savings, because then the college will come through with some money. Unfortunately, this strategy is impractical and is not recommended.

Start and Maintain a Manageable Savings and Investment Program

Chances are you will pay for some of the college bills and will be able to get loans as well.

Assume that you will pay for your child's education from a combination of savings, loans, and scholarship programs. And depending on your time horizon or how many years before your child will be ready to start college, you'll probably be able to accumulate a much larger sum than you think you can. While there are sound strategies for saving for college, there is no universal tactic that is right for everyone. You and your neighbor may have two children who are exactly the same ages, but each of you has different lifestyle priorities, unique attitudes about money, and varying comfort levels with risk. The one universal piece of advice for anyone who's saving for their kids' education: Start as early as possible.

Your first step should be to immediately put aside money, regardless of your child's age. In fact, as soon as your child is born you should set aside money for college. By starting early and saving money regularly, you're able to take advantage of the power of compounding, by which you continue to reinvest the interest your money earns. Unfortunately, as the parent of a newborn, you may feel particularly strapped for spare cash and can't imagine how you can find any unspent dollars after you pay all your bills. Perhaps you've just bought a new house or car and, if you and your spouse both worked before, one of you has stopped working.

While the prospect of saving may be overwhelming at this particular time, you know that you can do it. When you set your goal of buying a home, you had to adjust your spending and modify your budget in order to save enough for your down payment. Likewise, you need to include a college savings program in your budget. To do so, you will have to re-align your spending priorities. You will still need to have in place your emergency fund of three to six months of living expenses. And, obviously, you will continue to pay your monthly mortgage, utilities, and other fixed expenses. But you should still try to set aside some money for college, even if it's only a relatively small sum, say $25 each paycheck.

If, for example, you put aside $100 a month and earn an 8 percent annual compounded rate of interest, then in ten years you would have saved some $18,000, and in twenty years you would have saved nearly $57,000! That's pretty impressive. And, for some of you, especially if you live in an expensive metropolitan area, you could forgo one nice dinner or a night at the theater to set aside this money. Another strategy is to live on your current salary, not your higher one when you receive a raise. That is, when you get a raise, put the additional money into savings or investing rather than spending it. Likewise, if you inherit money or get an unexpected bonus, you will be able to add these funds to your college savings.

If your kids are old enough to understand the concept of spending and saving, you should involve them in your budgeting. For example, if you have a child in junior high and a newborn, you could talk about needing money for the older child's college education in five years. Explain to your child that you're trying to establish a college fund. Offer options: If you want to set aside more from each pay-check, see what your kids won't mind giving up. For example, they might decide they could do without a few dinners at a fast-food eatery but would rather not give up their video games. Talk about some of your plans; if you're thinking about postponing, say, a vacation or a new car, let your kids know the reasons behind this decision.

If you find that you're financially strapped when you have young children and absolutely cannot find any money to set aside for their education, you should still not panic. Let's say you have one child and a second on the way. You've been saving to buy a house, and you know that you'll have to move when the baby is born. Saving for that house is your top priority—for now. Focus on reaching that goal and then begin your college savings plan. In the future, your salary is likely to increase, so it will be easier for you to save more. Also, as a home owner, you will have the option of taking out a home equity loan to help pay for your kids' education.

Don't Put All Your Children's College Savings in Their Name

New parents often wonder whether they should be saving in their own name or that of their child. There are reasons for each method, but generally you should not put all your college savings in your child's name. When you open an account in your kid's name through a custodial account, through the Uniform Gift to Minors Act (UGMA) or the Uniform Transfers to Minors Act, depending where you live, the savings belong to your child. When your child reaches eighteen or twenty-one years of age, depending on the age of majority in your state, he or she can take the money. If the age of majority where you live is twenty-one, then by that time, your child will presumably have used most of the money for his or her education. However, at age eighteen, your child could simply take the money and spend it—on a trip to Europe, to join a cult, buy a car, or whatever. While you may be certain now that you will have instilled the right values in your child, there are no guarantees, and you will not be able to prevent your teenager from taking the money.

In addition, accumulating sizable savings in your child's name can hurt you if you were hoping to qualify for financial aid. Colleges generally expect that entering students will contribute 35 percent of their savings, but parents are expected to contribute only about 6 percent of their savings. So, if your child has $10,000 in savings, a college would expect $3,500 of that money to go for paying college bills. On the other hand, if you as a parent has $10,000, the college would expect you to use only $600. There is one clear advantage to saving in your child's name, especially when your child is young. If your child is under fourteen years of age, he or she will not pay any tax on the first $650 of investment income. The next $650 is taxed at the child's rate of 15 percent, which is much lower than yours. For children over the age of fourteen, any investment income is taxed at 15 percent. If you're fairly certain that you won't qualify for any aid because you're in a high tax bracket, then you may want to keep the savings in your child's name.

Where to Invest for College

You may remember as a child being given U.S. savings bonds by relatives who wanted to help you save for college. Savings bonds are still a useful way to save for college, especially if your income is below certain set levels. If you meet these guidelines and use the bonds to pay for tuition, you don't have to pay federal income tax on the bonds. However, savings bonds will now provide a smaller return. The Treasury has changed the way interest is calculated on savings bonds. For bonds issued after May 1,1995, the interest rate on the bonds will be adjusted every six months, and there is no longer a minimum interest rate. If you held a savings bond for seventeen years, you would be guaranteed to receive interest of just over 4 percent. However, that's a very low rate of return, especially if you're trying to pay for colleges whose costs are rising annually at nearly twice that rate.

If your child will not be starting college for another ten to fifteen years, you should be investing your money more aggressively. Stocks have outpaced the earnings of Treasury bills, bonds, and other investments, earning an average of 10.3 percent annually from 1926 to 1993, according to Ibbotson Associates, a Chicago financial firm. If stocks still make you nervous, perhaps because you lost money in the 1987 market crash, don't be so alarmed. With a time horizon of ten years or longer, you should be able to ride out any dramatic market swings.

Also, if you're uncertain about your ability to pick the right individual stocks for your college portfolio, you don't have to buy specific companies. Instead, you should look to mutual funds (see chapter 3). When you buy shares of a mutual fund, your money is pooled with that of other investors. The funds are run by a professional manager, so you can take advantage of his or her expertise in picking stocks. Also, investing in mutual funds for college is very easy. Since many mutual funds encourage investors to use funds to save for college, you may be able to buy shares with a modest initial investment as low as $50. Funds will often arrange for you to buy shares via an automatic withdrawal from a bank account.

Using an automatic withdrawal plan to invest is especially advantageous if you have trouble sticking to a budget or you occasionally go on spending binges. With the money going directly into the fund, you won't be able to use it for other purposes. Once you know that your bank account will be reduced by a set amount each month, then you have that much less money to spend on nonessential purchases.

You should look for growth and aggressive-growth stocks if you have a long time horizon. That way, you stand to earn as much money for your investment over time as possible. Experts advise that you own several funds to diversify your portfolio and limit your overall risk, but there's no reason for you to own dozens of funds. Assuming you have a long time horizon, you should divide your money as follows:

- About 75 percent of your money in two U.S. stock growth funds

- About 10 to 20 percent in an international fund
- About 5 to 10 percent in a bond fund

Remember, you're trying to earn as much money as you can for that ever-increasing tuition bill. But it's important that you consider how comfortable you are with market risk. If you're particularly cautious, you can settle for a slightly lower return by putting your money first in a conservative stock fund and then moving into a more aggressive growth fund.

You may want to switch funds depending on how a particular fund has been performing, but you shouldn't change your investment mix until about five years before your child will start college. When your child is in junior high, you should start to shift about half of your holdings into equity total return funds. When your child enters high school, you should begin to shift out of mutual funds. With only a few years until you will need the money, you can't afford to take losses if the market should suddenly decline. You should keep only about 10 percent of your money in stock funds, and, before your child finishes high school, you should have the rest of your portfolio in Treasury funds or certificates of deposit (CDs) of varying maturities so you can use the funds to pay the college bills.

Tuition Plans

You've probably heard about prepaid or guaranteed tuition plans. These plans, which were started in the 1980s, exist in several states including Florida and Pennsylvania. Under these plans, you can prepay tuition for one or more years at today's rate rather than whatever the college fees will cost when your child is ready to begin school. While the plans can save you money, you should consider them very carefully. If your child is starting high school and has his or her heart set on a particular school because of, say, a special program or the athletic department, then these plans may be a good deal.

However, if your child is a toddler, it's very hard to predict what college your child will want to attend. Some colleges will let you transfer the tuition payment to another college or refund your money, but you will not receive any interest on the funds. So it's possible that you will have tied up a fair amount of money without even keeping up with inflation. Also, when you prepay tuition, your child usually cannot apply for any scholarships or financial aid.

Scholarships, Loans, and Other Sources of College Funds

Even if you haven't accumulated as much as you wanted to pay for your children's education, your child should still apply to all the schools that interest him or her. You shouldn't limit your applications only to lower-priced schools. Talk to your child's college advisor to make sure you know about all scholarship or other programs that your child is eligible for. Also, make sure you carefully complete the Free Application for Federal Student Aid (FAFSA) early in your child's senior year of high school. Regardless of whether you think you will qualify for any financial aid, you must complete this form, which is used by colleges to award loans that are not based on financial need. The 1997 Tax Act included several provisions designed to help taxpayers pay for higher education. Among these provisions are:

- A $1,500 HOPE Scholarship tax credit covering tuition (not room and board) for the first two years of college for taxpayers earning less than $50,000 as single filers and $100,000 for couples filing jointly.
- Waiving of the 10% withdrawal penalty when funds from an IRA are used for college expenses.

- Establishment of a special educational IRA with a maximum contribution limit of $500 annually.

- A new interest deduction on education loans repaid within the first 60 months of required payments starting after December 31, 1997. The limit is $1,000 in 1998; $1,500 in 1999; $2,000 in 2000; and $2,500 in 2001 and years thereafter.

Here are some other sources of money for college:

Government loans There are still some loan programs that are open to anyone, regardless of their income. A program quite popular for parents is the Parent Loan for Undergraduate Student (PLUS), which lets parents borrow a sizable amount of money—the cost of college excluding any financial aid. You will pay an interest rate tied to the one-year T-bill plus 3.1 percentage points (adjusted annually) up to a maximum of 9 percent interest. The rate for 1994–1995 was 8.53 percent. You will also have to pay fees and up-front costs, which vary by bank. You will have up to ten years to repay the loan. Students can use the Stafford Loan Program to borrow up to $23,000 for their four years of study; they can borrow more money each year and have from ten to twenty-five years to repay the loan. (Information on government loan programs is in The Student Guide, available by calling 800-433-3243.)

Home equity loans Generally, you can borrow up to 80 percent of the value of your home, minus any outstanding mortgage. Interest on loans up to $100,000 is usually fully deductible. Take out a home equity loan cautiously, and make certain you will be able to handle the monthly payments on a home equity loan; if you fall behind, you could lose your home.

401(k) plans You can borrow from your employer's 401(k) plan. Depending on the rules of your plan, you may be able to borrow as much as half of your vested amount or $50,000, whichever is less. You will have to pay interest, usually the prime rate plus a point, and repay the loan within five years. The repayment is usually made through deductions from your paycheck. However, if you leave your employer before you repay the loan, you will have to pay taxes on the outstanding balance and a penalty if you're under age fifty-nine and a half. Also, if you're an older parent (over the age of fifty nine and a half) and your child is in college, you can withdraw money from your plan without incurring the early withdrawal penalty.

Money earned by your children Don't underestimate the value of a summer or part-time job for your teenagers. Depending where your child works, he or she could earn a thousand dollars or more, which could help close the gap between what you've saved and other aid money.

Special college programs Do your own research at a local library or consult with your child's college advisor. If your child is thinking about going to a school that you attended, see if any special breaks are given to children of alumni. If more than one of your children will be attending school at the same time, see if a school will provide a tuition reduction if they attend the same college. Some states offer special assistance if your children attend a state college rather than going to an out-of-state college. Check with your state office of higher education to find out if your state has this program.

Annuity and other insurance vehicles Some insurance agents will hype their products as a tool for college savings, but you should only borrow against these policies if you have no other sources of money. Life insurance is intended as protection of your family, not a means to pay your college bills. If you do borrow against a policy, make sure you understand the specifics of the loan and the impact on your policy.

Don't Give Up!

It's April 15, and you and your child have survived the stresses of selecting schools and applying to them. The good news is that your child has been accepted by his or her first choice. If you're less than thrilled, though, with the aid package that the college is offering, don't assume the decision is absolutely final. If your financial situation has changed—you or your spouse have been laid off; your house has been damaged by fire or a natural disaster; you are going through a divorce; or a family member needs treatment for a serious medical condition—contact the college. If you live nearby, see if you can schedule an appointment with a financial aid officer, and bring documents showing the changes in your finances. Otherwise, mail copies of these documents to the school. Explain that your child would really like to attend this school, but without additional assistance he or she probably will not be able to. There's no guarantee that the college will offer you more money, but you have nothing to lose by asking.

For more information on college finances, you should consult the following books, which are updated regularly:

- *The College Costs and Financial Aid Handbook* (College Board Publications)
- *Don't Miss Out* by Robert and Anna Leider (Octameron Press)

CHAPTER 7

TAXES

That old adage about death and taxes is true: You cannot avoid these eventualities no matter how hard you try. However, you can still make plans to handle both of these events. In chapter 8, you will find estate planning tips to help formulate a strategy for your family's well-being after your death. In this chapter, you will learn tactics that will make filing your tax return simpler. You will realize that while paying taxes may not be pleasant, it shouldn't cause you to have a mini-breakdown every year.

Like most Americans, you probably associate taxes with the need to complete and file your tax return by April 15 (or later, if you file for an extension). Sometime in January or February, you start digging out receipts, copies of last year's tax return, files, and other material that you hope will make the process easier. But you probably procrastinate, and as a result you leave everything until the last minute and frantically complete your return before the deadline. It is this ritual of avoidance that makes the notion of taxes so burdensome. However, taxes are simply another aspect of your financial planning. Instead of focusing solely on completing your return, you should begin to consider the tax consequences of all major investing and purchasing decisions that you make throughout the year.

TAX BASICS

By understanding some tax basics, you will be able to make keener decisions about your finances. Hopefully, these choices will enable you to keep more of your hard-earned money and reduce the amount of money you have to pay the Internal Revenue Service (IRS). First, though, you should have at least a rudimentary knowledge of the U.S. tax system.

When you hear about changes in the tax law or new IRS rulings, these regulations refer to federal taxes. Depending on where you live, you will have to pay state and city taxes as well (Alaska, Florida, Nevada, South Dakota, Texas, Washington, and Wyoming have no state income tax). Everyone must file a tax return, provided he or she earns over a minimum amount of money, as determined by the government. These amounts vary according to your age and marital status. A single person under the age of sixty-five earning more than $5,900 must file a return, and a married couple aged sixty-five and over filing jointly and earning more than $12,000 must file a tax return. Even if your gross income is less than the minimum level, you may have to file a tax return if you earn tips and your main source of income is Social Security.

If you've had the worst year of your life and are convinced you couldn't possibly owe the government any money, you still have to file. The IRS takes its deadlines quite seriously, and so should you. You need to file a tax return on time whether or not you owe the government any money. If you don't file or you file late, you'll be hit with a whopper of a penalty! The IRS imposes outrageous penalties—possibly as much as 75 percent of your tax liability—if you don't file. If you file but don't pay up, you'll be subject to late penalty fees, but these penalties are less than those imposed on nonfilers. If you need an extension to file your return, complete Form 4868, which will give you until August 15 to file your return. With this extension form, you will still have to make payment of your best estimate of what you owe the IRS.

Your Tax Bracket

Comparing your tax liability to that of your neighbors, friends, or parents is a waste of time. The IRS has made a number of significant changes to the tax rates, particularly in the sweeping Tax Reform Act of 1986. The current tax rates range from 15 percent up to 39.6 percent for the wealthiest taxpayers, and the income levels of the tax rates are adjusted annually for inflation. Your tax rate (also known as a bracket), along with your filing status and any exemptions and deductions you're eligible to take, determines your tax liability.

You will pay taxes on what is referred to as your taxable income. To determine this amount, you must first calculate your adjusted gross income, or AGI. Your AGI is your total gross income (including salary, interest payments, dividends, pension, etc.) minus certain business and investment losses and deductible contributions to retirement plans. To figure out the amount of money you owe taxes on, deduct any exemptions and deductions from your AGI.

The different filing categories are as follows:

- Single
- Married, filing separately

- Married, filing jointly
- Head of household

Forms

Now you know why you have to file. You've figured out what tax bracket you're in. But you keep hearing about the various forms that you have to complete. Don't worry: The IRS is fond of jargon, but once you translate the jargon and know which forms you have to complete, you will find completing your return less painful.

Your W-2 form is sent to you by your employer, and you should receive it by January 31. This form lists your name, address, Social Security number, your employer's tax identification number, and your income for the year. You will receive a W-2 from each of your employers. You will have to attach this form to your tax return; read the return to find out where your W-2 must be attached.

Form 1040 is the basic income tax form that you must complete. There are three types of 1040 forms; which one you use depends on your particular situation. About 70 percent of all taxpayers file the complete 1040, which consists of more than sixty questions and lets you list all tax credits and deductions you're eligible to take. (Along with the 1040 are many supplemental forms that you may have to file. Among these forms are: Schedule B to report interest and dividend income, Schedule C if you own your own business, Schedule D to report capital gains and losses.) If you are single and earn less than $50,000, you can file the 1040EZ, which is a simple one-page document. If your income is less than $50,000 but you have income from several sources, you can file 1040A, which is more detailed than 1040EZ but less complex than the standard 1040 form.

The IRS sends out forms to taxpayers each year, according to which forms you used the previous year. If you need additional forms or different ones, go to a local IRS office, library, or bank. If you have difficulty finding a particular form, call the IRS at 800-829-3676.

COMPLETING RETURNS

If you're single, only have one employer, and have few investments, you should be able to complete your own return. On the other hand, if you have income from several jobs, profits from selling a home, or more than one dependent, you may need help completing your return.

Don't be embarrassed to admit you're intimidated by the logistics of completing a return. You're in good company: About half of U.S. taxpayers get some type of help with their return. As a consequence, there's a booming business in tax help. There are many useful tax preparation guides from reputable accounting firms; software and even CD-ROMs are designed to help you complete your taxes. The IRS also provides help at local offices and hot line numbers, although it can difficult to reach these official help lines, especially as the April 15 deadline approaches. Free or low-cost assistance in your community is often available from retired accountants and other centers providing services for seniors.

If your return is especially complex, you may want to seek help from tax experts. Remember, though, that it's still up to you to do the preparatory work. Especially if you're paying for tax services by the hour, you don't want to show up with a box full of receipts. You should review last year's return and bring as much documentation—in some organized way so that you can find specific papers easily—as you think your preparer will need. There are several types of tax professionals you can consult:

Tax preparers These are people who are trained in completing tax returns and understanding the IRS regulations. The preparers are especially skilled at completing relatively straightforward returns for middle-income taxpayers. Also, while a tax preparer can accompany you to an IRS audit, he or she cannot represent you. Perhaps the most well-known tax preparation firm is H & R Block. Fees are generally quite affordable but will vary according to the complexity of your return.

Enrolled agents   These experts have worked as IRS auditors for at least five years and receive special training from the IRS each year. Their fees are higher than tax preparers, running on average several hundred dollars, but usually less than CPA fees. To find an enrolled agent in your community, you can call the National Association of Enrolled Agents at 800-424-4339.

Certified public accountants   A CPA is an accountant who has received certification based on passing several exams. CPAs generally handle tax returns for clients whose returns are complicated by large investments or business holdings. CPAs will usually charge you an hourly fee, although some will charge a flat rate for certain services. Look for a CPA who belongs to the American Institute of Certified Public Accountants (AICPA). To find one in your area, call the AICPA at 800-862-4272.

Tax attorneys   These are attorneys who are experienced in tax matters, such as audits and new IRS regulations and court rulings. Tax attorneys generally advise clients on tax planning issues throughout the year rather than simply focusing on completing tax returns. Attorneys charge hourly fees that can run as high as $400 per hour.

Before selecting any specialist, be sure you understand his or her fee structure and how much you will have to pay to have your return completed. Make sure the fee includes state and local income taxes if you have to file these forms as well. Also, find out whether the expert will accompany you to an IRS audit. You should also ask about the preparer's experience. Some preparers have other full-time jobs and simply prepare returns to supplement their income. Look for someone who has several years of experience completing returns.

Experts advise you to keep all your tax records for seven years from the date of each return, in case you are audited. In some instances, you should keep older tax records as well—keep returns for any years in which you bought or sold a house, for example. Other records such as loan statements and contractors' receipts should be saved for as long as possible. Having these bills will enable you to prove the amount of money you spent on home improvements, to figure out the cost basis of your home when you sell it.

THE DREADED AUDIT

Although the IRS has been auditing more returns in order to increase its revenue—an estimated 450,000 audits will be conducted this year—this still represents only about 1 percent of all tax returns, so you shouldn't worry about whether you'll be audited. Instead of worrying about whether you'll be audited, you should concentrate on filing your return on time and keeping your backup documents available in the unlikely event the IRS questions your return.

The IRS can investigate your return in several ways. Most of the audits are correspondence audits, in which you are asked to supply documentation by mail. (Send the IRS copies of your documents; never send in the originals.) Or you could be audited in an IRS office. You're given notice ahead of the appointment, and the IRS tells which areas it is reviewing so that you can bring the appropriate documents with you. Sometimes, the IRS will come to your home or office to conduct a field audit. In this case, all of your return is subject to questions.

Remember, too, that you have rights if you're audited. The IRS publication *Your Rights as a Taxpayer* spells out your rights when the IRS is questioning your return. Among your rights: You are entitled to have a representative come with you to an audit, you can offer to pay disputed taxes in installments, and you can appeal the findings of an audit.

LOOK FOR WAYS TO CUT YOUR TAXES

If you're now thoroughly fed up with the subject of taxes, keep in mind this important message: Your taxes are a year-round component of your personal finances. Don't try to understand the latest IRS ruling or master the intricacies of the tax code. Instead, you should focus on understanding the tax implications of your financial decisions.

If you run your own business, you're already well aware of your obligations as a business owner and the resulting tax consequences. Even if you're a salaried employee with only a small savings account and few investments, you can benefit from knowing IRS regulations. For example, in December your employer offers you a choice of receiving your bonus that month or early the following year. While it's tempting to take the money to pay for holiday gifts, that may not be your best option. If you think that you will be in a higher tax bracket—earning more money—next year, then you may not want to postpone taking the money until the next year.

You know that putting aside money in an individual retirement account (IRA) or other retirement account is a good way to postpone taxes. But did you know that you can deposit money in a Keogh (retirement account for self-employed people) up until April 15, provided you open the account by the previous December 31? And, in one of the rare instances of generosity by the IRS, if you're buying or selling a home, you're eligible for many very favorable tax breaks.

Hopefully, you're already following the advice in chapter 1 and have started organizing your financial files and papers. If so, you're well on your own to gaining control over your taxes. Not only will having your receipts and other documents in some organized file help you and/or your tax preparer when you do file your taxes, but reviewing these records will make it easier for you to weigh your investment and other financial decisions. Then, you can make choices that are more favorable to you instead of the IRS. And, after all, isn't that the name of the game—you don't want to pay the IRS any more than you have to!

Once you understand your tax bracket and what you've paid in taxes over the past few years, you can begin to think about what changes in your spending, saving, or investments would cut your tax bill. To help you devise these strategies, you should certainly ask your accountant or tax preparer, if you've used one. Or you can call the IRS (800-829-3676) and ask for a list of free publications. The IRS publishes myriad pamphlets on topics such as depreciation, tax guide for small business, moving expenses, and selling your home.

Some key issues to consider:

Self-employment You work for yourself and you're dismayed at how much of your income you have to pay in taxes. You're wondering if you should work less and thereby pay less in taxes. You shouldn't think in terms of working less (unless, of course, you're ready for a lifestyle change) but rather in what ways you can reduce your taxable income by taking more deductions.

You should make certain you're taking all eligible deductions, including your home office, travel costs to and from client meetings, etc. While there has been a great deal of publicity about the IRS disallowing the home office deduction, you should still consider taking one provided you meet all the IRS guidelines for this deduction.

Investments   You will have to pay capital gains taxes on investments that you sell. But you can reduce this liability by selling off portions of your investments. If you own, for instance, 1,500 shares of stock in one company and want to sell 500 shares, ask your broker to sell off the 500 shares that you paid the most for. This way, you'll pay less in taxes. Or if you've had a terrific year with all your investments bringing in money, you should consider selling off investments that haven't performed as well. That way, you can offset some of your profits with losses.

Convert nondeductible consumer debt   It's in your best interest to pay as little consumer interest as possible, since this debt is no longer deductible. Provided you have your spending under control, consider taking out a home equity loan or second mortgage to pay off this nondeductible debt. Interest on home equity loans and mortgages is still deductible, in most situations.

Selling a home   There are several ways you can take advantage of the IRS regulations on home sales. You can postpone paying taxes on any profits you make from selling your home provided you buy another home for the same or more money within twenty-four months. For sales of homes after May 7, 1997, you can exclude up to $250,000 of gain ($500,000 if you're married and filing a joint return). You can use this exclusion once every two years, provided you have lived in your home for at least two of five years before the sale. In certain circumstances—including medical reasons or change in employment—you are entitled to a partial exclusion even if you haven't met the two-year requirement.

Tax-free/tax deferred investments Assuming you can afford to put aside money, you should take advantage of investments that allow you to postpone paying taxes or avoid paying them all together. If you are in a high tax bracket and also pay state taxes, consider buying tax-exempt bonds. You don't have to pay taxes on the interest you get from these bonds; in some instances, you are exempt from state tax as well.

Although the IRS has made the guidelines on IRA deductions stricter, you still get a tax break by depositing your money in an IRA. Contributions to an IRA reduce your gross income, thereby lowering the amount of money you owe taxes on. If you're covered by a 401(k) plan through your employer, you should also utilize the plan to the fullest, because these plans offer you excellent tax savings. Like an IRA, any money you put in these retirement plans reduces the amount of your income. In addition, you don't have to pay taxes on any interest, dividends, or other gains in your 401(k) investments until you withdraw the money.

Charitable contributions Don't overlook your good deeds. You can deduct donations provided you get an itemized receipt from the charity for all donations over $250. Also, if you're a particularly active volunteer, you can deduct expenses you have that are related to your volunteer position. If you have to buy a uniform or regularly drive to and from the charity location, you can deduct these expenses.

Income shifts Consider reducing your tax bill by making gifts of your money. You can give up to

$10,000 to anyone, a friend or relative, without incurring any tax liability.

New businesses   Provided you can show the IRS that you have a sideline business that you started with the intent to make money (you don't want the IRS to label your business a hobby), you can deduct various expenses involved in setting up the business, such as travel, home office, and entertainment. Be prepared, though, to document all the steps you've taken in order to make the business profitable.

Chapter 8

Estate Planning

How many people spend any time thinking about their own mortality? It's too depressing, and after all, you reason, why worry about something that is inevitable? In fact, you'd probably do almost anything to avoid making plans about what will happen after you die or write your will. It's estimated that more than half of all Americans die without a will. That means an alarming number of people are making a serious mistake. While you won't be around for the consequences, your loved ones will.

Everyone should have a will, regardless of the amount of savings and property they own. While some money—from insurance policies or retirement accounts, in which you have named a beneficiary—will go directly to the person you have named, the rest of your estate will be divided by the state if you don't have a will. A will is a legal document that spells out how you wish to have whatever you own divided. By having a will, you can decide who gets what, rather than having the state or the IRS divide your possessions. And it's highly unlikely that you and the IRS would agree on how your estate should be split among your family and friends.

If you die intestate—without a will—not only is it likely that your family will have to wait a long time before they can get any of your property, but your family has no say in who gets your property. For example, if you have a common-law spouse, when you die, your parents and/or siblings will be entitled to your property, not your mate, unless you have a will. In many states, if you die without a will, your children will get the majority of your estate, not your spouse, even if your children are babies. Your children are another key reason why you need to have a will: You can name guardians for your children should something happen to you.

ESTATE PLANNING BASICS

The mere mention of estate planning may send you running the other way in fear. Or you may shrug and say that you're too poor to worry about what happens to the few meager possessions you have. Estate planning, while not a pleasant task, is a necessary one for everyone. To help you get started, here are some basic definitions:

> **Will** A will is a legal document in which you spell out what you want done with your possessions and who will take care of your underage children.

> **Intestate** This simply means someone who has died without a will.

> **Executor** The executor is a person you name to supervise your estate and carry out your wishes, as expressed in your will.

> **Probate** This is the legal process of distributing your estate, as supervised by probate court.

Property Whatever you own is your property and part of your estate. This property can be real, such as a house or land, or personal, such as money, clothing, stocks, etc.

Gift This is something that you freely give to someone; not a sale.

Trust This is a legal arrangement whereby you transfer assets to someone else to hold for the benefit of someone you name as beneficiary.

GETTING THINGS IN ORDER

As depressing as it is, you have to consider what would happen if you or your spouse suddenly passed away. If you have already written a will, is there a copy at home that someone in your family could find easily? Do you have a list of your insurance policies, bank accounts, stocks, and other investments? You also have to consider whether there's an emergency fund available to cover your family's day-to-day needs. Even if your will is straightforward and there are no complications, your family may not have access to your estate or even to insurance money. You should maintain an account that will cover funeral expenses, probate (the legal splitting of your estate) fees, as well as your family's living expenses for several months or longer if possible, since probate can take anywhere from several months to a year or more.

Important Documents

You should keep your valuable documents, such as the deed to your house and your insurance policies, in one place at home. Other papers that should be accessible include your birth certificate, cemetery deeds, and Social

Security card. You should also include a list of the names and addresses of your lawyer, accountant, and broker, as well as relevant data about family members, especially the names and ages of minor children. You should also keep a copy of your will at home, with a close relative, or at your attorney's office. If the original of your will is in a safe deposit box, your survivors may not be able to open the box without a court order.

Although it is not legally binding, you should also consider leaving a letter of instruction for your survivors. This letter can alleviate some of the stress on your family as they sort out your finances and other matters after you die. This letter should be kept with other valuable papers and can include instructions about your funeral, whom to notify upon your death, a listing of debts, etc.

Durable Power of Attorney

You should also decide who you would like to make decisions about your finances should you become physically or mentally unable to make these decisions yourself. Known as a durable power of attorney, this is a legal document in which you name someone else as the person who will handle your finances. A durable power of attorney can be "special," giving someone limited power such as writing checks, or "general," which covers all circumstances.

Living Will/Health Care Proxy

Doctors, lawyers, the clergy, and countless others are continually debating ethical issues raised by advances in modern science. If you have known someone who was or is being kept alive through artificial means, you know how difficult a situation this can be. Because hospital policy on such treatment varies, you should try to protect yourself with two documents. With a health care proxy, you designate someone who can make decisions about your medical treatment if you are not conscious or cannot do so yourself. In a living will, you state whether or not you want to be kept alive by artificial means.

USE AN ATTORNEY, BUT DECIDE WHAT YOUR WILL SHOULD SAY

Do you need to consult an attorney or can you write a will yourself? While there are several first-rate do-it-yourself will books, you probably should consult an attorney to avoid any chance that your will won't hold up in court as a legal document. There are laws governing the distribution of property and the taxes on estates, so don't assume that the lawyer who handled your house closing can write your will.

You should hire an attorney who is familiar with estate planning and the laws in your state. As with hiring other professionals, you should ask friends or colleagues for recommendations. Or you can call a local bar association for the names of attorneys who specialize in estate matters. If your will is not complicated, your attorney will charge you from $250 to $750, depending on where you live. You will pay more if you have a great deal of property or other complicated bequests. A good estate lawyer should do more than assist you with your will; he or she should offer advice on using trusts or other ways to pass on your property without having to pay a hefty portion to Uncle Sam in taxes.

Read this chapter before you consult an attorney to draw up your will. Deciding how you want to distribute your property isn't always simple. Any advance planning on your part will help your attorney. Before visiting your lawyer, make sure you know exactly what assets you need to account for in your will. Find out in whose name are various accounts—bank, mortgages, stock certificates, etc. Bring this information with you to your lawyer. You'll save both time and money by having this information and thinking about how you want to divide your assets before you consult with the attorney. Ultimately, you want your will to accurately represent what you want done with your estate.

To write a will, you must be at least eighteen years old and of sound mind. If you don't have a will, draw one up as soon as possible. Remember those old movies in which the family gathers around a yellowing piece of handwritten paper to hear what ninety-year-old Grandpa finally left them? It may work in the movies, but a will must be typed in order to be legal in all fifty states. On rare occasions, a handwritten (holographic) will is considered legal. A video-taped will, while helpful to the family, is not legally binding. Your will should be typed and stapled together with the pages numbered. Depending on where you live, you will need two or three witnesses. The witnesses should not be beneficiaries of the will and the witnesses only have to see you sign the will. There is no reason for them to read the document.

If you already have a will, you should review it periodically to make revisions that may be necessary because of changes in your life. If you have children and have gotten married or divorced, you probably will have to rewrite your will. You should also revise your will if your financial circumstances have dramatically changed or if there have been major changes to the tax laws. You can amend a will with codicils. Like your original will, you will need to sign these amendments with witnesses present. You can add on several codicils to your will, but if you are making substantial changes, you should probably rewrite the entire will. Never cross out or scratch out sections of your will; this could make the whole will invalid.

EXECUTORS AND GUARDIANS

Be ready to name an executor of your estate in your will. An executor has a number of important duties in carrying out your wishes. This person is in charge of paying your debts and taxes, having your assets appraised, distributing your property, and collecting any money that is owed to you.

The executor has to appear in court, where he or she is officially designated as such. Unless you specify in your will that you don't want a bond collected, the executor is usually required to post a bond of the value of the estate (the bond premium will come from the estate) to show the executor's good faith that he or she won't make off with the assets of the estate.

The executor will carry out what you have requested in your will, but will also have to use his or her discretion in some matters such as whether to sell off certain assets promptly or keep them. Therefore, it's important you pick someone who is both capable and has the time to serve as executor. You can name a spouse or an adult child as executor, or you can hire a lawyer or banker as executor.

An executor generally gets paid a fee ranging from 3 percent to 5 percent of the value of the estate. Presumably, a family member would not take this fee. However, if your estate is large or complicated, you can consider naming two people as coexecutors, perhaps a family member and a banker. If you name a family member as executor, that person can hire someone to help at a later time.

Though not required by law, you should try to find an executor who lives in the same state as you. The executor goes to court before distributing your property and again after all the property has been distributed to let the court know that your estate is closed. It is up to probate court to declare your estate closed, assuming no challenges have been made. This is where the probate process can be lengthy.

An executor is not the same as a guardian. A guardian is someone who will raise your underage children until they reach the age of eighteen. Obviously, deciding who will raise your children is a sensitive issue, which you and your spouse will have to discuss at length. In fact, it is this decision that prevents many people from writing a will. You may want to name your brother as guardian, but your spouse insists that his or her parents are much more responsible. You have to sit down and calmly evaluate your options. The bottom line: You want to name someone in whom you have absolute faith and confidence, who you know will be able to raise your children if you aren't around to do so.

You should consider issues like where the guardian lives, whether your children get along with that person or couple, and whether you agree with their opinions and lifestyle choices. If you're thinking about naming your parents as guardian, think about whether they are physically capable of handling the demands of young children. Be sure you talk to the person and ask whether he or she feels comfortable with the responsibility that can come with being named a guardian. It's natural to avoid thinking that you won't be around to raise your children until they're adults, but there are no guarantees. You know that you don't want the state to take the children and put them into foster care. You owe it to your children to name a guardian.

WHAT BELONGS IN YOUR WILL

Other sections of your will should cover these topics, if applicable:

- Distribution of specific personal effects, such as jewelry, artwork, etc.

- Exclusion of certain family members from inheriting anything
- Name of executor
- Name of guardians if your children are under the age of eighteen
- Details about any trusts that have been established
- What assets should be used to pay death taxes or other debts (maybe you'd prefer that stock be sold instead of personal property)

OTHER ESTATE CONSIDERATIONS

Some additional pointers about your will. Although you should update it periodically, it's possible that you won't do so. Therefore, it's better to specify what portion of the estate you would like someone to get. For example, while you may want to leave $5,000 to your young grandson now, you might feel differently in a few years depending on how much money you have in your estate and what your grandson is doing. If you want to leave someone money but are uncertain how large your estate will be in the future, you may want to phrase the inheritance in another way. Talk to a lawyer in these circumstances.

Both spouses should have a will, not only the primary breadwinner in your family. Without two wills, the family situation can get tangled if the surviving spouse dies shortly after the first spouse's death. In this case, without a will, the state will then decide how to split up the estate. In fact, some attorneys urge you to insert a "simultaneous death clause." This may sound macabre, but it is really a standard clause in a will, which specifies that if it can't be determined who died first, then the property of each spouse should be disposed of as if he or she survived the other.

This insures a distribution that is in keeping with the wishes of both spouses.

If you're separated but not divorced, and you die, your spouse is entitled to a certain percentage of your estate, according to state law. Regardless of what you say in your will, if your spouse were to contest the will, the state would have to award this minimum amount. Certainly, if you're planning to divorce, you should change your will so that your spouse gets only the minimum as required under your state's law. Again, you should consult an attorney to find out the law in your state.

Obviously, someone is likely to be unhappy with your will. Perhaps some relative feels he or she is entitled to more money or property. More likely, your children may be unhappy with the way you have split up your property. While it's not possible to avoid these conflicts, you can try to lessen the possibility that people will be angry and try to contest the will.

If you're planning to exclude one of your children, for example, you might try to explain why. You don't have to put this in the will—which after all is a legal document and open to public examination. But you can in your letter of instruction state something to the effect that you leave one-third of your estate to your daughter because she is a doctor and has a comfortable income and you're leaving two-thirds of your estate to your son who is a struggling artist. No doubt your daughter will still be irritated but at least you've expressed your wishes.

Some lawyers suggest you talk to your children or other relatives, tell them ahead of time what you're planning, and get their reaction. You can, obviously, try to have a reasonably calm discussion, but you should be ready to proceed as you see fit if your children are not happy when you tell them what you plan to do. If you're planning to leave your house to your three children in equal shares, talk to them ahead of time. While they may say that it seems fine, there are also likely to be squabbles, even if you leave them equal shares. When you introduce the issue, perhaps one of your children will say that he or she has no interest in the house and it should be split between the other two siblings. The discussion may not resolve the issue, but you may be pleasantly surprised if someone offers you a solution that you hadn't considered.

If you're leaving money to a child who is married, you can specify that you are leaving whatever money or property to the person as separate property. This means you want your child to own the property rather than your child and his or her spouse jointly.

If you move after you have written your will, you don't have to write a new one. However, if you own houses in more than one state, you will essentially have to go through two probates to meet the laws in each state before you can sell or divide the property. Again, a lawyer should be able to tell you what taxes you will be responsible for in both states.

TAXES

Death doesn't end your obligations to Uncle Sam. You, or rather your executor, must still file any outstanding federal and state income tax returns.

Estate tax is federal tax due on estates larger than $625,000 (increasing by $25,000 each year until the exemption reaches $1 million in 2006) paid at rates ranging from 37 percent to 55 percent. It must be paid within nine months of your death. Remember that even if beneficiaries have been paid life insurance or other premiums, these amounts must be added to determine the dollar value of your estate. If you and your spouse die together and your combined estate does not exceed $1.5 million, you don't have to pay federal estate tax.

One way to reduce the size of your estate is to give gifts to family members. You can give anyone up to $10,000 annually without having to pay taxes. Also, you can make tax-exempt gifts without a maximum amount for certain medical treatments or school tuition. You cannot, however, just write your grandchild a check for school. You must make payment directly to the college or other school or pay a hospital directly for treatment of a relative.

If you want to leave your entire estate to your spouse, regardless of its size, you can do so, and your surviving spouse will not have to pay any federal estate tax. However, you probably don't want to do this if you want children or other family members to receive some money in the future. Rather than leave your entire estate to your spouse, you should consider setting up a trust that will provide your spouse with income to live on during his or her lifetime, then allow the remaining money to be passed onto children or other beneficiaries.

TRUSTS

Having a will means taking a vital step in protecting your assets. Another strategy that your attorney may advise you to consider is setting up a trust. Don't assume that trusts are only used by the very wealthy. A trust is simply an arrangement in which you turn over your assets to someone else to manage (the trustee); you specify who will get any income, as well as the holdings of the trust (the beneficiaries). To set up a trust, you will need to consult an attorney. You will also have to pay a fee to set up the trust and also pay annual fees to maintain it.

The most common types of trust are:

Testamentary trust These are trusts you create in your will and fund with the assets of your estate.

Living trusts These are trusts you set up for use while you're still alive. If you're ill, you can create a revocable living trust by which a trustee handles some or all of your financial matters. Then, if you recover, you can revoke the trust and resume handling your own finances. However, revocable trusts are subject to income and estate taxes. Only irrevocable trusts, whereby the assets are controlled by the trust itself, are excluded from income and estate tax.

Marital trust This type of trust allows you to protect your assets from the long arm of the IRS. Suppose a spouse inherits his or her spouse's entire estate. When this person dies, the entire estate (over the $625,000 amount) would be subject to estate tax. If, however, a trust existed, providing income to the surviving spouse and leaving the remaining money to children or other surviving family members, then tax would not be owed. With a general power of appointment trust, your spouse would be able to choose who gets the trust's assets when he or she dies. Under a qualified terminable interest property (QTIP) trust, you decide who will get the trust's assets when your spouse dies.

Bypass testamentary trust If you become incapacitated or die, up to $625,000 of your assets can be put into this type of trust. Your spouse will receive income from the trust and, if you specified in the trust, a portion of the principal, 5 percent of the principal, or $5,000 (whichever is greater) annually. If your spouse requires additional money for medical purposes, the trustee can also provide this money. When the spouse dies, your children become the trust's beneficiaries. This trust isn't subject to estate tax, because the $600,000 is within the amount excluded from estate tax and the trust is not part of the surviving spouse's estate.

Irrevocable life insurance trust With this trust, you transfer ownership of your life insurance policies to a trust. When you die, the proceeds from the policy go into a trust, which will provide income to your spouse. When your spouse passes away, the life insurance trust goes to whomever you have named in the trust agreement. A warning, however, about these life insurance trusts: If you die within three years of setting up this type of trust, the proceeds become part of your taxable estate. To get around this, you should specify that the proceeds should go directly to your spouse or into a trust if you die within the three-year period.

Another way to reduce your assets that are subject to estate tax is to establish a charitable remainder trust. There are various types of these trusts, but you can establish one to provide a beneficiary such as a spouse or child with an annuity for life with the assets or property actually going to a charity.

Trust Planning

Before setting up any type of trust, consult a lawyer and accountant who are experienced in this field. You should also make sure you understand all the tax ramifications of your decision. Trusts can be very useful devices to pass on property as well as reduce estate taxes. They can have a fair amount of flexibility.

These arrangements can be especially advantageous in today's era of nontraditional families. It's not uncommon for people to be in a second marriage, with each spouse having children from their previous marriages. Setting up a trust is a way to protect assets that you want to pass to your children from the previous marriage rather than your present stepchildren.

For example, you can set up a "special needs" trust to help a child that is mentally or physically handicapped. Or you can give the custodian "sprinkling" rights, which allow the custodian to use part of the trust's principal for certain expenses such as college tuition or medical bills. Or, if you're worried about whether a child or other relative will make good use of the money, you can establish a "spendthrift" trust, which doesn't allow the beneficiary to touch the principal ever, or until a certain age.

Uniform Gifts

Sometimes, though, you can protect your estate in ways other than setting up a trust. For example, if your assets are relatively modest, say under $25,000, then you can probably use the Uniform Gift (or Transfers) to Minors Act, which allows you to leave property or money to your children with a custodian in charge of the property until your children reach the age of eighteen. You can name yourself custodian, but you should also name a successor custodian to take over if you die.

The key difference between uniform gifts and other trusts for children is that the custodian can only have control of the property until your children reach the age of majority. However, for relatively small sums of money, this is fine, because the custodian may in fact use up some of the money by the time the child reaches eighteen. Furthermore, gifts transferred in this fashion are taxable and must be reported to the IRS.

OWNERSHIP

Depending on how you own your home, car, and other big-ticket items, passing these items to your heirs can be simple or a hassle. Obviously, if the property can be passed onto someone else without having to wait for the probate for the estate, that's preferable. Generally, when you own property with another person, the property can pass to the other person without having to go through probate.

For example, let's say you own a boat with your brother, in "joint tenancy with right of survivorship"; if you die, your brother automatically owns the boat. Regardless of other wishes you may have, because of the joint tenancy, your brother gets the boat. Another form of ownership, "joint tenancy by the entirety," operates under the same principle, but it applies to husband and wife. In both these cases, the signature of both people must be on the title or deed of the property.

Another form of ownership is tenancy in common. Let's say you own 50 percent of a summer house. On your death, your 50 percent share would pass to whomever you specified in your will. In this case, the house would be subject to probate, and the named heir would have to wait for probate to be completed before getting access to his or her share of the property.

Another consideration is where you live. If you live in a community property state, such as California, almost all property acquired during marriage is considered joint property. So, if one spouse dies, the other spouse is entitled to half of that person's share of the community property, and the remaining half can be left to someone else.

PLAN FOR YOUR LOVED ONES TODAY

While there are legal requirements regarding wills, inheritance, and probate, these rules may conflict with your own moral or emotional positions. The worst thing you can do is to do nothing. Although you may feel that you absolutely can't make the right decision—whether to name one person over another as guardian or whether you should leave your children equal shares of your estate— you need to make the best choices you can and write a will. No doubt you want your legacy to be a lasting and loving one. You won't be around to see whether it is, but you should know that your preparations at least reflect your own best decisions. You owe that much to your heirs.

CHAPTER 9

RETIREMENT: PLAN TODAY FOR TOMORROW

You may be counting the days until you can retire, while your spouse refuses to even say the word retirement. You can't wait until you can spend all the time you want on the golf course or out sailing; meanwhile, your spouse is planning to start a new career. You may want to move out of your house to a small condo across the country, but your spouse intends to stay put. Today, retirement consists of a variety of lifestyles that may or may not include a job, depending on your financial, psychological, and physical needs. While the notion of retirement varies from one person to another, virtually everyone is worried about their finances for the retirement years. Nearly three-quarters of the people who consult a financial planner for the first time do so because they are most concerned about their retirement funding, according to a survey of financial planners conducted by the National Endowment for Financial Education.

Regardless of what you expect to do once you retire, it's important that you start planning for your retirement years as early as possible. More than one-quarter of the population over age fifty-five hasn't started saving for retirement. If you fall into that category, you'd better slap your wrist and begin a crash savings and investment program today! And if you're part of the baby boom generation and intend to keep working for many years, you should already have a solid retirement plan in place. Baby boomers are only saving at an embarrassingly low 36 percent of the rate they should be saving for their retirement, according to the Merrill Lynch Baby Boom Retirement Index.

You may wonder why your parents didn't worry as much about their retirement. Most of your parents and grandparents worked for one employer throughout their career and were left with a sizable pension. Unfortunately, many of you are not so lucky. Not only are company pensions smaller and less secure, roughly half of all American employees have no pension plans because they have worked for several companies and therefore haven't accumulated enough years to qualify for vesting in a pension plan. Also, with life expectancies now at 72.8 years for men and 79.7 years for women, if you retire at age sixty-five, you could well live another twenty-five years. If you live longer, a combination of savings, investments, pension funds, and Social Security will have to stretch farther than it did for previous generations. Furthermore, inflation, while relatively low during the 1990s, will diminish the buying power of your funds. An additional concern is whether the Social Security system is secure. While the system is not about to go bankrupt, there's a good chance that legislative changes will reduce benefits to many recipients within our lifetime.

GAUGING THE AMOUNT YOU'LL NEED

Whether you're planning to retire in five years or not for another fifteen to twenty years, you should first determine how much money you will need to live on. It's hard to answer this question, especially if you're uncertain where you'll be living, whether you'll be working part-time, whether you'll be in good or poor health, or how you'll be spending your time. However, even with these variables unanswered, you can still estimate what you'll need to maintain a lifestyle that's comparable to your present one. You should assume that you will need from 60 percent to 80 percent of your current income to live on when you retire. For most middle-class and upper-middle-class Americans, Social Security will provide less than one-third of these funds. Assuming you have either no pension or a very small one, you will need to accumulate enough in savings and investments to fund your retirement and provide you with ongoing income if you choose not to work when you retire. As you begin to calculate how much money you need, you can see whether your retirement goals are reachable. If you have accumulated much less in savings, then you may have to continue working longer or alter some part of your retirement plans. On the other hand, if you're still a decade or more away from retirement, by investing some of your money more aggressively you may be able to reach your goal easily.

START EARLY

As with investing for other goals, it's essential you start investing for your retirement as soon as possible. If you're already putting aside 10 percent to 15 percent of your income in a variety of investments, you're taking the right steps toward a comfortable retirement. The key is starting to set aside money early and regularly. If you invest $2,000 for ten years with an 8 percent return, then at the end of thirty-five years you will have accumulated $212,295. If your spouse starts putting aside $2,000 for twenty-five years, starting the year after you stop putting aside money, he or she will only have accumulated $157,909, in spite of having set aside $50,000.

First, to get a handle on your retirement savings plan, here's a worksheet to help you do some calculations (tables follow workwheet).

Dreyfus Retirement Planner Worksheet

1. Current annual income before taxes.

    $_____

2. Annual income you will need during retirement.
    (Assume between 60% and 80% of current income.)

    $_____

3. Adjust the amount in Step 2 for inflation.
    (Under the 4% column in Table 1, select the amount that appears next to the number of years you have until retirement. Multiply this figure by the amount in Step 2.)

    $_____

4. Total current retirement savings.
    (Include IRAs, SEPs, Keoghs, 401(k) accounts, and other investments specifically set aside for retirement.)

    $_____

5. Value of the amount listed in Step 4 at retirement.
    (In Table 1, find your number of years until retirement and select an assumed annual rate of return on your investments until retirement based on a fair assessment of your risk tolerance. Circle the amount that lines up with these two figures, then multiply it by the amount in Step 4.)

    $_____

6. Annual cash flow (principal and investment income) you could receive throughout retirement from savings listed in Step 5.
    (In Table 2, find your expected age at retirement and select the assumed rate of return on your investments during

retirement. Circle the amount that lines up with these two figures, then divide the amount in Step 5 by this figure.)

$_____

7. Annual projected Social Security retirement benefits.
(In Table 3, circle the amount listed to the right of the year you were born. Enter this amount for an individual. If you have a nonworking spouse, multiply this figure by 1.5. If both you and your spouse are eligible for Social Security, multiply this figure by 2.)

$_____

8. Social Security retirement age adjustment.
(In Table 4, find your expected age at retirement and select the assumed rate of return, during retirement. Circle the amount that lines up with these two figures and multiply the amount in Step 7 by this figure.)

$_____

9. Annual pension benefits.
(Indicate the amount you expect to get during your first year of retirement. Check with your Human Resources department if necessary.)

$_____

10. Additional income you will need annually during retirement.
(Add the amounts from Steps 6, 8, and 9, then subtract that total from the amount in Step 3. A negative amount means you have sufficient pension income/retirement savings to meet your stated retirement income needs.)

$_____

11. Additional savings you will need by the first year of retirement to supply the income listed in Step 10.
(Select the figure you circled in Table 2. Multiply it by the amount in Step 10.)

$_____

12. Retirement savings you must set aside each year until you retire.
(In Table 5, find your number of years until retirement and select the assumed rate of return until you retire. Circle the amount that lines up with these two figures, then divide the amount in Step 11 by this figure.)

$_____

TABLE 1

Years Until Retirement	Assumed Rate of Return				
	4%	6%	8%	10%	12%
5	1.22	1.34	1.47	1.61	1.76
10	1.48	1.79	2.16	2.59	3.11
15	1.80	2.40	3.17	4.18	5.47
20	2.19	3.21	4.66	6.73	9.65
25	2.67	4.29	6.85	10.83	17.00
30	3.24	5.74	10.06	17.45	29.96
35	3.95	7.69	14.79	28.10	52.80
40	4.80	10.29	21.72	45.26	93.05

TABLE 2

Age at Retirement (if married, use age of younger spouse)	Assumed Rate of Return				
	4%	6%	8%	10%	12%
50	39.42	27.10	19.68	15.00	11.90
55	34.62	24.81	18.57	14.45	11.63
60	29.81	22.30	17.24	13.74	11.24
65	25.00	19.53	15.63	12.79	10.68
70	20.19	16.48	13.68	11.53	9.86

TABLE 3

Year You Were Born	Maximum Projected Social Security Benefits with Assumed Age of 65 (Individual)
1930	$14,388
1935	$19,041
1940	$24,274
1945	$30,724
1950	$38,393
1955	$47,210
1960	$58,045
1965	$70,620
1970	$85,921

TABLE 4

Age at Retirement (if married, use age of younger spouse)	Social Security Adjustment				
	4%	6%	8%	10%	12%
50	0.35	0.30	0.25	0.20	0.16
55	0.49	0.44	0.39	0.34	0.30
60	0.69	0.66	0.62	0.58	0.54
65	1.00	1.00	1.00	1.00	1.00
70	1.22	1.22	1.22	1.22	1.22

TABLE 5

Years Until Retirement	Assumed Rate of Return				
	4%	6%	8%	10%	12%
5	5.63	5.98	6.34	6.72	7.12
10	12.49	13.97	15.65	17.53	19.65
15	20.82	24.67	29.32	34.95	41.75
20	30.97	38.99	49.42	63.00	80.70
25	43.31	58.16	78.95	108.18	149.33
30	58.33	83.80	122.35	180.94	270.29
35	76.60	118.12	186.10	298.13	483.46
40	98.83	164.05	279.78	486.85	859.14

Worksheet reprinted courtesy of Dreyfus Service Corporation. Copyright 1995, Dreyfus Service Corporation.

The Dreyfus Retirement Planner Worksheet is intended to serve only as a very generalized tool to assist you in your retirement planning activities. IT IS PROVIDED TO YOU "AS IS" WITHOUT WARRANTY OF ANY KIND. The calculations produced by the Worksheet are only general estimates relating to your future savings based up168on a variety of apparent assumptions. Also, the tables are for illustrative purposes only and are not intended to predict the performance of any investment. As a result, the actual return on your investments will vary, in most cases significantly, from the results generated by the Dreyfus Retirement Planner Worksheet. Dreyfus Service Corporation encourages you to consult with a qualified tax and/or financial advisor concerning the results generated by the Dreyfus Retirement Planner Worksheet.

EARLY RETIREMENT

What if you haven't been giving much thought to setting a date for your retirement? You're fifty-five years old, in reasonably good health, and enjoy your job. Unexpectedly, your employer offers you an early retirement package. Should you take the money and run? First of all, don't let your employer rush you into making a hasty decision. Ask for enough time to evaluate the pros and cons; if your employer is offering counseling, take advantage of the opportunity and talk to the advisors.

Assuming you have already done a retirement planning worksheet (see the previous section), you will have to recalculate some of the variables. Here's a guide to the key issues:

- How much pension will you be getting? While your company may be adding "bonus years" in order to calculate your pension benefit, you should look carefully at your final payout. You have to find out how your pension plan determines this figure. If, for example, it is based on your average salary for the last three to five years of working, then by taking an early retirement, your pension will not be based on the higher salary that you would presumably be earning if you kept working. On the other hand, if your salary only increases negligibly or just keeps pace with inflation each year, then adding bonus years to calculate your pension may provide you with close to what you would otherwise get if you kept working. Furthermore, some companies will add other sweeteners so that your pension payout matches what it would be if you continued to work. You should review your plan carefully and talk to a company representative to determine how much money you are losing (or, occasionally, gaining) by taking an early retirement package rather than continuing to work.

- Is your company going to provide health benefits? You are not eligible for Medicare until you reach age sixty-five, and medical coverage for you and your spouse can cost as much as $1,000 a month. Therefore, if you cannot arrange coverage through your spouse's employer if he or she is still working, then ask whether your employer is willing to pay for all or part of your health insurance or at least arrange for you to pay a reduced group rate. Alternatively, look into less costly coverage through a local HMO.

- How much of your savings are tied up in retirement plans? If you have to take money out of these plans before you reach age fifty-nine and a half, you will incur substantial tax penalties. Generally, if you take out money from your 401(k), IRA, or other tax-deferred savings plan, you will have to pay a 10 percent penalty as well as taxes on the withdrawal.

- Social Security payments do not begin until you reach age sixty-two. And, at that age, you will receive a reduced portion of your benefits.

Don't forget to consider your own lifestyle preference. If you're healthy and enjoy your job, you may not be psychologically ready to retire. A temporary break from the daily grind of a full-time position may be appealing, but if you're accustomed to working, a forced early retirement may not be pleasant, regardless of how attractive the financial package is.

RETIREMENT FUNDS

You have three sources of money available for your retirement: Social Security, pensions, and savings and investments. The following sections will examine each of these categories in detail.

Social Security

Social Security, which was started back in 1937, was designed as a way to pay back workers for all the taxes they had paid while they were working. During the early years of the system, the benefits were quite substantial and often provided the sole support for retirees. Today, however, Social Security benefits are smaller and will provide less than 30 percent of the money you will need to live on when you retire. Assuming that you earn close to the maximum income subject to Social Security tax ($60,600) and you collect benefits at the full rate at age sixty-five, you will get about $14,000 annually. If you and your spouse both work, you will get just under $28,000. If only one of you works, you will get about $20,600 each year. These benefits are adjusted annually for inflation.

Remember, though, you may have to pay taxes on your Social Security if you have other income from interest and earnings. You will have to pay taxes on 85 percent of your Social Security benefits if your modified adjusted gross income and half of your Social Security is more than $44,000 (for married couples) or $34,000 (for singles and heads of households). And, if you work, you have to give back money ($1 for every $2) you earn over $8,160 if you are between the ages of sixty-two and sixty-four. If you are between sixty-five and sixty-nine, you have to give back $1 for every $3 you earn over $11,280.

You should find out how much money you can expect in Social Security benefits (in fact, it's a good idea to check your earnings record every few years to make sure that you're being properly credited for all your working years). To get an estimate of your benefits, call the Social Security Administration at 800-772-1213 to get a copy of Form SSA-7004, a Request for Earnings and Benefit Estimate Statement. Mistakes—usually because of similar names or use of incorrect Social Security numbers—do happen, and you should call or visit your local Social Security office if you think there's been an error in calculating your earnings.

To qualify for Social Security on your own, rather than collect as a spouse, you must have worked forty quarters or roughly ten years. If you start to collect at age sixty-two, your benefits will be permanently reduced by about 20 percent of the full benefit you would have gotten had you retired at the normal retirement age of sixty-five. However, in part because of the underfunding of the system, the normal retirement age is rising. By the year 2027, age sixty-seven will be the normal retirement age. Also, if you postpone retirement, your benefits are upped by 4 percent for each year beyond age sixty-five up until you turn seventy. After age seventy, your benefits are not increased.

Pension Plans

Employers, including the government, offer a variety of pension plans. You can also fund plans yourself, if you own a business or are not covered by a plan through your employer. The plans vary by how much you can put in them, where the money is invested, how payouts are made, whether the pension funds are fully guaranteed, etc. Generally, there are very tight restrictions on withdrawals. While you may be able to take loans for emergency situations, you should expect to incur a 10 percent penalty if you withdraw money from these plans prior to age fifty-nine and a half.

As with most investments, your pension money is not 100 percent safe. After all, companies do go bankrupt, and some pension money is put into speculative investments that also go bust. Fortunately, most pension plans are secure, and the plans are regulated by the government. Under ERISA (Employee Retirement Income Security Act), you are entitled to receive a copy of your pension plan rules as well as annual updates on the money in the pension fund. The two major types of pension plans are:

Defined benefit plan In these plans, your employer determines how much money you will get when you retire. Generally, you will have had to work for a company for at least seven to ten years in order to qualify for the full benefits. The benefits are based on how long you've worked for the company, your salary, and other factors. These plans have become less prevalent, because many employers cannot or do not want to pay out pensions to all employees.

Defined contribution plans Both you and your employer contribute to these plans, which have become increasingly popular. Your employer can set aside a maximum of $30,000 or 35 percent of your salary, whichever is less, each year. When you retire or leave the company, you receive a lump-sum payout of your plan holdings. The most common type of defined contribution plan is the 401(k) plan.

You can set aside roughly $9,240 or up to 13 percent of your gross salary, whichever is more, into your 401(k) plan each year (the amounts are adjusted annually for inflation). In addition, about one-third of companies with 401(k) plans match employee contributions, from 25 percent to 100 percent, up to 6 percent of the employee's salary. Most employers kick in $.50 for every dollar you contribute to the plan. This is too good a deal to pass up, but roughly one-quarter of those eligible for a 401(k) did not participate in 1994. If your company matches some portion of your contribution, you're essentially getting free money. Also, since you are making pretax contributions, your taxable income for the year is reduced (your federal tax is reduced and your state and local taxes may be reduced as well, depending on where you reside).

Taxes on your 401(k) holdings are not due until you withdraw the money. Employers used to offer only three options, including stock in the company, but increasingly employers offer as many as ten investment choices, including mutual funds, guaranteed investment contracts (GICs), and other options. As companies add to the investment options available through a 401(k) plan, some employers provide financial consultants to help employees evaluate their options. Sometimes investment seminars are held at company sites. In other cases, your employer may hire a large financial service firm, such as Fidelity, to offer "lifestyle products." Under these plans, you select the category of fund you're interested in, and the firm makes the final choice.

It's important that you keep in mind your non-retirement investments when you're making your 401(k) choices. Don't limit yourself to GICs, which are the most conservative option. You should look to more aggressive investments, including international funds, especially if you are planning to work for twenty or more years.

Just as you evaluate your investment choices outside of your retirement funds, you should not be intimidated by the many options. Certainly, you don't want to put your retirement money at risk, but you also don't want it earning virtually no return. You should carefully evaluate the fund families to look for equity funds, especially if you're more than ten years away from retirement. Stocks have returned an annual average return of 10.3 percent after inflation over the past sixty-eight years, according to Ibbotson Associates (see chapter 3). This far exceeds the return on cash and bonds.

Remember too that stocks are meant to be a long-term investment. Don't get rattled by day-to-day movement in stocks. You should aim to hold onto your stock funds unless there is a dramatic change, such as a sharp drop in earnings or a new fund manager. Look at funds that hold different-size companies: generally, mid-size to larger companies are less volatile than funds holding smaller companies. One rule of thumb, according to some investment experts, is to subtract your age from 100 to get the percentage of your holdings to put into stock. So, if you're twenty-five, then 75 percent of your portfolio should be in stocks.

Don't forget that if you leave your company before age fifty-nine and a half, you must roll over the 401(k) money into another retirement plan at your new employer or into a rollover IRA. If you don't make these rollovers, you will be subject to a 10 percent early withdrawal penalty as well as taxes on your holdings. Some companies let you keep your 401(k) funds with them after you leave the company. If the investments have been performing well and you don't think you could do better investing the money on your own, then you may want to leave the money in your employer's plan. Most 401(k) plans also allow you to borrow money from your holdings, which can help if you need some emergency funds.

If you are self-employed or own a small business, you should set up your own pension plans. You have two basic choices. With a Keogh money purchase plan, you can contribute up to 25 percent of your self-employment income, up to a maximum of $30,000, whichever is less. You must set up a Keogh plan by December 31 in the year in which you want to take the deduction, but you can continue to make contributions until the following April 15 or later, if you file for an extension on your taxes. Some paperwork is needed to manage and administer your Keogh.

Simplified Employee Pension plans (SEPs) operate much like an IRA. Your contributions accumulate tax-free until you withdraw the money. You can put more into a SEP than into an IRA; you can put in 15 percent of your net earnings or $22,500, whichever is less. SEPs can be set up anytime up to the day you file taxes. You can keep your SEP at a bank, brokerage, or mutual fund company. If you run a small business, when you set up an SEP, it must be available to every employee, even part-time workers. An SEP has no vesting rules; employees are entitled to their holdings when they leave the company.

Individual Retirement Accounts

Since the IRS changed the regulations and began to limit the use of IRA investments as deductions, these accounts are sometimes overlooked as a retirement investment vehicle. They are still a good place to put your money, because the money accumulates on a tax-deferred basis. You can contribute to your IRA until April 15 when you file your tax return, but opening your account earlier in the year will give you a greater return. However, the money is no longer fully deductible for everyone. You are still entitled to a full or partial deduction if you are single and have an adjusted gross income less than $35,000 or you are married and your AGI is less than $50,000. One tip: If you have both deductible and nondeductible IRAs, keep the accounts separate.

As with other benefit plans, if you withdraw your IRA holdings prior to turning fifty-nine and a half, you will have to pay a penalty and taxes. However, if you die, your beneficiary will not have to pay the 10 percent penalty. You have to start to withdraw your money by April 1 following the year you turn age seventy and a half. Withdrawal rules can be confusing, so you should ask your banker or broker to help you decide how to calculate your life expectancy to figure out how much to withdraw at a time.

Annuities

A newer retirement investment option that has been getting a lot of attention is the deferred annuity. The annuity lets you set aside money for your retirement that accumulates on a tax-deferred basis. You have a variety of choices when considering annuities. With fixed annuities, you receive a flat specified interest rate; your principal and minimum interest rate is guaranteed. With a variable annuity, you put your money into bonds, stocks, and other investment options. While your money may grow substantially, there's also a risk that you will lose all or some of it.

There is no limit to what you can put into an annuity. However, you should first fund the aforementioned retirement vehicles before getting an annuity. In addition to early withdrawal penalties if you take the money from your annuity before you turn age fifty-nine and a half, you will also have to pay steep surrender fees—as high as 8 percent—if you take out your money after holding the annuity for less than ten years. In addition, annual fees usually average around 2 percent, slightly higher than many mutual funds.

If you are interested in an annuity, shop very carefully. Look for highly rated insurers and ask about all expenses, surrender charges, and other fees.

YOUR RETIREMENT PORTFOLIO

As you approach your retirement, you will have to start shifting your portfolio holdings. Obviously, your choices will be based on your retirement plans, your risk tolerance, the size of your portfolio, and other considerations. The following advice is meant to provide some general guidelines only.

If most of your money has been in growth funds, you should begin putting some of this money into growth and income funds about five to ten years before your retirement. Your holdings should be roughly split between growth and income funds and bond funds, with about 20 percent in money market funds. As you get closer to retirement, you should assume that you will need to use some of your holdings to pay for your living expenses. Also, you don't want to invest in high-risk funds, because you no longer have the luxury of a long time frame to withstand a very volatile market. Keep roughly one-third of your holdings in money market funds, one-third in bond funds, and one-third in growth funds.

FINAL POINTERS

To ease your transition into retirement, here are just a few more invaluable tips:

- If you have not already done so, make sure you and your spouse have investigated long-term care insurance and have also discussed issues related to caring for your elderly parents. While these can be unpleasant issues, they must be faced, and the sooner you confront them, the better off you'll be.

- Don't wait until the last minute to apply for Social Security benefits. You should apply three months before the date you want to start collecting your benefits.

- Evaluate your life insurance. If your children are grown and living on their own, you may not need to have as much life insurance as you reach your middle years and approach retirement.

- Review your will.

- If you're planning to sell your home and are at least fifty-five years old, make sure you understand the tax implications.

- Begin to get information on other regions that you're thinking about moving to. Take a vacation or spend a month in another community before you make a decision to retire there.

APPENDIX 1

HOW TO FIND A FINANCIAL PLANNER

By following the advice in this book, you should be able to get your finances on firmer ground and start working toward your long-term goals. Depending on your income, aspirations, and lifestyle, you may be able to handle your finances on your own. However, if you are having trouble sticking to a budget or establishing a long-term plan, you may need to consult a financial professional.

As with any decision concerning your money, you should first arm yourself with as much information as possible. You should draw up a list of your assets and liabilities and complete an account of your spending habits (even if you're not following a budget) before you talk to a planner. You should also carefully investigate the background of any advisor you're considering hiring. You wouldn't think twice about comparison-shopping if you were buying a new computer or joining a health club, so don't get lazy because you're hiring a so-called expert.

Don't assume that someone who calls himself or herself an advisor is experienced and reliable. There are several designations used by financial planners as well as different ways that planners bill their clients. You shouldn't look for a planner in your Yellow Pages. After all, it's your money, so you should hire a competent and experienced professional that you feel will look out for your interests.

There are three key terms used by planners to explain their fees. The distinctions are fairly straightforward:

Fee only   These planners charge client fees, either by the hour or on a fixed rate. Fees vary by planner but generally range from $100 to $250 per hour or from several hundred dollars to $10,000 for a complete financial plan.

Commission   These planners receive a commission on the financial products—insurance, mutual funds, annuities—they sell. When you get advice from commission planners, consider the advice carefully, since the planners are making money on the products you buy. Commission charges vary depending on the type of product you're buying.

Fee/Commission   A hybrid planner charges a fee to prepare your financial plan and also charges you commissions on the products you buy. Some planners adjust their fees, depending on the products you buy.

Almost anyone—accountant, lawyer, broker—can say they're a planner and offer their services to other people. However, the most reliable planners have received some training and accreditation from professional organizations. Here are the most commonly used designations:

Certified Financial Planner (CFP)   Planners who are a CFP have passed a lengthy exam given by the CFP Board of Standards, part of the College of Financial Planning, a nonprofit industry group based in

Denver, Colorado. In addition, CFPs must take thirty hours of courses every two years.

Chartered Financial Consultant (ChFC) The American College in Bryn Mawr, Pennsylvania gives this designation to insurance agents who have taken extensive courses and have experience with financial planning. Insurance agents can also get the CLU, or Chartered Life Underwriter, designation.

Accredited Personal Finance Specialist (APFS) This is a designation used by certified public accountants (CPAs) who have experience in personal financial planning and have taken an exam.

Money Manager Anyone can trade securities by filing form ADV with the Securities and Exchange Commission and paying a $15 fee. No additional training is required by law, although money managers generally handle larger portfolios for a fee of between 5 percent and 25 percent of the assets. Before hiring a money manager, ask to see his or her ADV to review the manager's history and fee schedule.

Do Your Homework First

You can ask friends or other professionals such as your lawyer or accountant to recommend a planner. Then, you should talk to these advisors to see whether you would be comfortable having them help you manage your money, regardless of whether you have a specific problem or want someone to manage your entire portfolio. Before selecting an advisor, you should find out the following:

References Ask the planner for names of clients or other professionals like attorneys or accountants who refer clients to the planner. If the planner isn't willing

to provide these references, take your business elsewhere.

Fee schedule   Ask the planner for a specific break-
out of all charges. If the planner is a fee-only planner,
ask whether the fee is an hourly rate or a fee per financial plan. If the planner receives commissions, find
out what the commissions are per type of transaction,
such as mutual fund transactions or stock purchases.

Experience   Find out how long the advisor has
worked as a planner. Ideally, you'd like to find someone with at least five years of experience.

Number of clients   Ask how many clients the planner has. A planner with many clients can still be a good
one, but you should find out ahead of time whether you
will meet with the planner or an associate.

Type of clients   If you have a modest income and
relatively small amounts of money to invest, you don't
want a planner whose clients have million-dollar portfolios. Ask the planner about his or her clients and
what size portfolios the planner typically handles.

Education   Find out whether the planner has any of
the professional certificates and whether the planner
participates in other ongoing educational programs.

Most planners will be able to handle a wide range of
financial situations. However, if you have a particularly
sticky problem, you may want to find a planner who has
handled similar problems. For example, if you are handling finances for elderly relatives, including someone who
requires nursing or long-term care, see if you can find a
planner who has elder care experience. On the other hand,
if you use a specialist such as an insurance agent or a
stockbroker, don't expect this person to provide advice on
other areas of your portfolio such as estate planning.
During or prior to your first meeting with a planner
you will have to complete a balance sheet so that the

planner understands your current assets and liabilities. He or she will also need to know about your credit history and your current investments as well as your future goals, such as whether you're saving for a new house or retirement. The planner should discuss these goals and explain whether your financial plan matches these goals. Together, you should examine all aspects of your financial history, including your insurance policies, estate plans, taxes, etc.

After several meetings, the planner should present a written assessment of your finances and specific suggestions for steps you should take. Some planners will refer you to other professionals, such as an attorney or tax accountant. Unless the planner is a broker, he or she will make specific investment recommendations and then refer you to a broker or mutual fund.

If you ever have an unpleasant experience with a physician, even if it isn't life-threatening, you probably would switch doctors. Similarly, don't assume that your relationship with a financial planner has to be a permanent one. If you're unhappy with the advice your planner provides or the investments he or she selects, then you should ask for explanations. If you're still dissatisfied, then you should terminate the relationship.

While you may find it difficult to "fire" your planner, you should not delay if you have concerns about how the planner has handled your money. After all, it is your money that is at risk. If you're worried about the performance of your investments and believe your advisor is not acting in your best interests, you should end the relationship without delay. Send a registered letter, return receipt required, to the planner. If you think that your planner should be held responsible for monetary losses, you should consult an attorney.

There are some warning signs that may indicate your planner is not acting in your best interest. Look for the following:

- You cannot reach your broker or planner easily. Your calls are not returned promptly, even when you indicate you're calling about an urgent matter.
- Your advisor is not carrying out your agreed upon investment strategies. He or she is buying stocks that you don't want to buy or making more trades (known as churning in the brokerage industry) than you have authorized.
- Your investments are steadily losing money, and your advisor has not been switching your money to other investments.

While it's more difficult to check on pending complaints against a broker, you can find out if there has been a final judgment against a complaint by calling the National Board of Standards and Practices for Certified Financial Planners at 800-322-4237. For problems with brokers, call the National Association of Securities Dealers at 800-289-9999.

If you have difficulty finding a planner in your area, you can contact professional associations to get a list of planners in your community:

International Association for Financial Planning (800-945-4237): Members of this organization must have three years of experience and meet other standards.

Institute of Certified Financial Planners (800-322-4237)

National Association of Personal Financial Advisors (800-366-2732): This is an organization of fee-only professionals.

APPENDIX 2

CONSUMER HELP

Following are some key names and addresses that you will be able to use when you run into problems with a particular product or service. This source list is not comprehensive. Consumer rights is an important subject that merits detailed explanations of how to solve a variety of problems. There are shelves of books about effective complaining and how to get companies to listen to the consumer.

Some basic tips for handling problems:

- Remain calm and composed. You may be furious that your new pants shrunk in the dryer, but screaming obscenities to a company operator won't solve the problem. Channel your anger into a phone call or letter explaining the problem and what you feel is an effective resolution. If you're not getting any results, then you can continue to complain, perhaps in a more public way, to embarrass the company into listening to your complaints.

A possible exception to this rule is when you've receiving such bad service that you want to create a "public scene" so that your complaint can be handled immediately. There's no guarantee that it will work, but guests who found that the hotel didn't have a room, even though reservations were made, have been known to create a disturbance in the lobby so that the manager will be forced to make some arrangement.

If you have a problem, try to complain immediately. If you're on vacation and there's difficulty that isn't the fault of the hotel or the airline but is due to errors made by your travel agent, then you may have to wait until you get home. But, for example, if you arrive at a hotel and are given a dirty or noisy room, insist that you be moved to more acceptable accommodations as soon as possible. Don't waste your vacation fuming and cursing the hotel management. Depending on how your complaint is handled on the scene, you may want to follow up when you get home, but if speaking up immediately can alleviate the problem, you should do so.

• Unless you're too busy or the problem is over a few pennies, you should complain. Most companies want their customers to be happy and will make some effort to ensure that the customers are satisfied. If you open a box of cookies and find they're stale, don't just throw them out. If the grocery store won't provide a refund, contact the company. See if there's a toll-free number listed on the package. If not, then write a brief letter to the company, and if possible, enclose the UPC code from the package. Chances are the company will send you a refund check or coupons to cover the purchase or another product.

• Don't assume that legal action is your best recourse. You should first try to solve complaints by going back to the store or other vendor involved. Then go to the manufacturer, then a trade association or consumer group. You should consider going to small claims court or filing a lawsuit only after other efforts to resolve the problem have failed.

• Do your homework when you're making a major purchase or other commitment of time and money. When you join a health club, for instance, read the fine print so you know under what circumstances you can cancel your membership and whether you'll have to pay a cancellation fee. If you're buying furniture, find out ahead of time the store's policy on delivery, assembly, and damages.

CONSUMER ORGANIZATIONS

Council of Better Business Bureaus, Inc.
4200 Wilson Blvd.
Arlington, VA 22203
703-276-0100

This is the national headquarters of the nonprofit Better Business Bureaus, which operate throughout the country. You can contact the headquarters to get free consumer bulletins and find out the location of the nearest BBB to your home. Local BBBs often have hot lines and provide information about the complaint records of businesses. If you're having difficulty resolving a complaint against a particular company, you should contact your local BBB.

National Foundation for Consumer Credit
8701 Georgia Avenue, Suite 507
Silver Spring, MD 20910
301-589-5600

This nonprofit group operates local debt counseling services designed to help you work out repayment plans with your creditors.

Call for Action (CFA)
3400 Idaho Avenue NW
Suite 1101
Washington, DC 20016
202-686-8225 (Tuesday to Friday, 11 A.M. to 1 P.M.)

This consumer action group has been solving problems and alerting consumers to fraud for more than thirty years. If you've been victimized and need help, write to CFA and explain the problem, including copies of any related receipts and documents.

National Fraud Information Center
800-876-7060

Run by the National Consumers League (NCL), this center passes along consumer complaints to government agencies and will also make suggestions to resolve the problem.

Automotive Consumer Action Program (AUTOCAP)
8400 Westpark Drive
McLean, VA 22102

For new car problems that dealers won't resolve, contact AUTOCAP, which represents a dozen car manufacturers, including Honda, Saab, and Nissan.

INDUSTRY GROUPS

American Society of Travel Agents (ASTA)
1101 King Street
Alexandria, VA 22314
703-739-2782

Booklets on avoiding scams and traveling safely are available from this trade association. In addition, you can get lists of agents in your community. If you feel you've been treated unfairly by a travel agent, you should notify ASTA as well.

U.S. Tour Operators of America (USTOA)
211 East 51st Street, Suite 12B
New York, NY 10022
212-750-7371

If you are arranging a trip through a tour and want to make sure the tour operator is legitimate, contact the USTOA to see whether the tour operator belongs to this organization.

Mail Preference Service
Direct Marketing Association (DMA)
P. O. Box 9008
Farmingdale, NY 11735

Members of this organization sell through direct mail, telemarketing, newspapers, etc. If you would like to have your name removed from mailing lists, contact this organization.

American Automobile Association
1000 AAA Drive
Heathrow, FL 32746-5063
407-444-7000

This organization has branches throughout the country. For a membership fee, you get emergency towing services, discounts, and other benefits. AAA will also help mediate some disputes between consumers and car dealers.

GOVERNMENT

Federal Trade Commission (FTC)
Sixth Street & Pennsylvania Avenue NW
Washington, DC 20580

The FTC has jurisdiction over a wide range of industries and companies from mail-order businesses to retailers to funeral homes. Although the FTC won't resolve an individual complaint, you should still notify the agency, because if other consumers have been defrauded as well, there may be a settlement for everyone.

U.S. Postal Service
Chief Postal Inspector
475 Le'Enfant Plaza SW
Washington, DC 2026-3100
202-268-4299

If your complaint involves something sent through the mail, you should notify the U.S. Postal Service.

Federal Communications Commission (FCC)
Enforcement Division, Common Carrier Bureau
2025 M Street NW
Washington, DC 20554

For problems with phone service, especially long-distance service, write to the FCC.

APPENDIX 3

RESOURCES

F ollowing is a list of organizations, associations, and other sources of information on financial and related consumer affairs. These brochures and newsletters are usually available for free or for a nominal charge. For information on virtually any topic, you should check with the Consumer Information Center in Pueblo, Colorado, which has thousands of publications. Other government agencies also have useful material, although you may have some difficulty requesting the material by phone; for example, the IRS has many free publications that can be helpful if you're running a small business. The Social Security Administration also provides booklets on its services. Also, don't overlook your local library; reference librarians can steer you to directories that list industry organizations, company headquarters, and other resources.

FINANCIAL PLANNERS

Council of Better Business Bureaus, Inc.
4200 Wilson Blvd., Suite 800
Arlington, VA 22203
703-247-9310

This umbrella organization for the BBB publishes many useful consumer brochures around the country, including *Tips on Financial Planners* ($1 and a self-addressed stamped envelope).

National Association of Personal Financial Advisors
1130 Lake Cook Road, Suite 150
Buffalo Grove, IL 60089
800-366-2732

This organization publishes *Fee-Only Planners* and *Questions That Could Change Your Financial Future*, which may provide useful information.

National Endowment for Financial Education
4695 South Monaco Street
Denver, CO 80237-3403

Wealth Care Kit is a group of fact sheets designed to help you get a handle on various personal finance basics, including estate planning, budgeting, and retirement. The kit is available free.

INSURANCE

Insurance Information Institute
110 William Street
New York, NY 10038
212-669-9200

Nine Ways to Lower Your Auto Insurance Costs, Taking Inventory, Home Security Basics and other brochures are available free. For general questions or help resolving insurer problems, call the Insurance Information Helpline at 800-942-4242.

INVESTING

Securities and Exchange Commission
Office of Consumer Affairs
450 Fifth Street NW
Washington, DC 20549
202-942-7040

Invest Wisely: Advice From Your Securities Industry Regulators includes advice on selecting brokers and handling disputes with brokerages. Other publications cover mutual funds and pyramid schemes.

Investment Company Institute
1600 M Street NW
Washington, DC 20036
202-387-6121

An Investor's Guide to Reading the Mutual Fund Prospectus walks you through the basics of a fund prospectors. Other publications on closed-ends funds and using mutual funds to save for college are also available.

Oppenheimer Management
800-892-4442

Women and Investing is available free and has useful tips, especially for fledgling investors.

Mutual Fund Educational Alliance
1900 Erie Street, Suite 120
Kansas City, MO 64116

The Investor's Guide to Low-Cost Mutual Funds lists
nearly 1,000 mutual funds that you buy directly from the
fund company (include a $7 check).

Merrill Lynch
Local offices nationwide

Ninety-Five Tax-Planning Ideas for Investors offers tips on
changes in the tax law, income shifting techniques, gift
taxes, etc. Call your local office.

REAL ESTATE

American Homeowners Foundation
6776 Little Falls Road
Arlington, VA 22213-1213
800-489-7776

Mini Guide to Home Ownership is a free booklet with tips
to help you decide whether or not you really want to own
a home.

HSH Associates
1200 Route 23
Butler, NJ 07405
800-UPDATES

*ARM Check Kit: How to Verify Your Interest Rate Adjust-
ment* is a guide to making sure your adjustable-rate mortgage is calculated accurately. Other brochures on home
equity loans and refinancing are available ($3 check).

RETIREMENT/ELDER CARE

Consumer Information Center
Pueblo, CO 81009

What You Should Know About Pension Law (Booklet 365B)

American Association of Retired Persons (AARP)
Worker Equity
601 E Street NW
Washington, DC 20049

A Guide to Understanding Your Pension Plan (Stock #D13533)

National Center for Women & Retirement Research Group
800-426-7386

Booklets, worksheets, and videos are available.

National Academy of Elder Law Attorneys
602-881-4405

Information is available on finding an elder law attorney.

Eldercare Locator
800-677-1116

Provides help in finding local services to assist you or an elderly relative.

Consumer Information Center
Department 40
Pueblo, CO 81009

Social Security ... What Every Woman Should Know is available free.

Pension Benefit Guaranty Corporation
Public Affairs, Room 700
2200 K Street NW
Washington, DC 20006-1860
202-778-8840

Your Pension: Things You Should Know about Your Pension Plan and *Your Guaranteed Pension* are free publications.

SAVING MONEY/SPENDING WISELY

U.S. Office of Consumer Affairs
1620 L Street NW, Suite 700
Washington, DC 20036

Consumer's Resource Handbook is one of the best freebies available. It includes tips on how to resolve consumer disputes, company addresses, arbitration and resolution panels, and more.

Consumer Information Center
Department 39
Pueblo, CO 81009

66 Ways to Save Money is a brochure covering many topics from travel to banking. Available for $.50.

Consumer Information Center
Pueblo, CO 81009

Too Good to be True! lists government and private agencies that will help if you've fallen for some type of scam (Booklet 597B).

Federal Reserve Bank of New York
Public Information Department
33 Liberty Street
New York, NY 10045
212-720-6134

A Penny Saved, The Story of Money, etc. are comic books about saving, the history of banking, and the U.S. banking system. They are useful for elementary-age children.

Credit Union National Association
Public Relations
Box 431
Madison, WI 53701

Checking is a free booklet on managing your checking account. Send a self-addressed stamped envelope. Request a list of other publications; this association publishes helpful booklets on other topics, including car leasing.

National Foundation for Consumer Credit
800-388-2227

kids & money is a free newsletter for parents needing help teaching their children about money and the best use of credit. Available from local offices. Call for the location of the nearest office.

Bankcard Holders of America
524 Branch Drive
Salem, VA 24153
703-389-5445

Low-Rate/No-Fee List is a survey of banks across the U.S. that offer credit cards with no annual fee and low interest rates. Other publications from this nonprofit organization cover gold credit cards, secured credit cards, and managing your money ($4 for Low-Rate).

Consumer Task Force for Automotive Issues
Box 7648
Atlanta, GA 30357-0648

Reality Checklist is a tipsheet telling you how to read between the lines of an auto lease ($1 check and self-addressed stamped envelope).

VISA
800-VISA-511

Credit Cards: An Owner's Manual is an unbiased beginner's guide to buying on credit. It's available free.

Federal Trade Commission
Public Reference Branch, Room 130
Sixth Street & Pennsylvania Avenue NW
Washington, DC 20580
202-326-2222

How to Dispute Credit Report Errors and *Credit Repair Scams* are free booklets.

American Financial Services Association
919 Eighteenth Street NW
Washington, DC 20006
202-296-5544

Consumer Budget Planner and *What You Should Know Before Declaring Bankruptcy* are full of useful advice on these topics; free with a 4-by-9-inch self-addressed stamped envelope. Other booklets on credit, money and your marriage, and a budget calendar are available for modest charges.

Aetna Life & Casualty Co.
800-906-7233

10 Minute Crime Safety Audit offers tips on making your house more secure against burglars. It's available free.

National Center for Financial Education
P. O. Box 34070
San Diego, CA 92163
619-232-8811

How to Choose a Travel Agent and other brochures on credit topics are available from this nonprofit organization ($1 for travel agent brochure).

Overseas Travel Advisory Hotline
202-647-5225

If you're traveling abroad and are uncertain whether the area you're going to is safe, call this State Department hot line.

Good Advice Press
Box 78
Elizaville, NY 12523
800-255-0899

Stop Junk Mail ($3) and other publications are available. They also publish a quarterly newsletter, *The Pocket Change Investor,* with tips on saving money in all areas of your financial life.

Consumer Information Center
Department 133-B
Pueblo, CO 81009

Fly Rights ($1.75) is an update booklet from the Department of Transportation on the latest rights of airline passengers.

RECOMMENDED READING AND SOFTWARE

Following is a list of publications and software that will provide additional assistance in managing your finances.

Banking and Credit

The Bank Book: How to Revoke Your Bank's "License To Steal"—And Save Up to $100,000 by Edward F. Mrkvicka, Jr. (HarperPerennial)

Checkbook Management: A Guide to Saving Money by Eric Gelb (Career Advancement Center)

The Complete Idiot's Guide to Managing Your Money by Robert K. Heady and Christy Heady (Alpha)

Downsize Your Debt: How to Take Control of Your Personal Finances by Andrew Fineberg (Penguin)

The Personal Budget Planner: A Guide for Financial Success by Eric Gelb (Career Advancement Center)

The Ultimate Credit Handbook: How to Double Your Credit, Cut Your Debt and Have a Lifetime of Great Credit by Gerri Detweiler (Plume)

Software: *Banker's Secret Loan Software* (Banker's Secret; 800-255-0899)

Estate Planning

Loving Trust by Robert A. Esperti and Renno Paterson (Viking)

Own It and Keep It: How to Reduce Your Taxes, Preserve Your Assets, and Protect Your Survivors by Theodore H. Hughes and David Klein (Facts on File)

Software: *Nolo's Living Trust* (Nolo)

Financial Planning

The ABCs of Managing Your Money by Jonathan D. Pond (National Endowment for Financial Education)

Everbody's Money Book by Jordan Goodman (Dearborn)

Personal Finance for Dummies by Eric Tyson (IDG Books)

Smart Ways to Save Money During and After Divorce by Victoria F. Collins and Ginitia Wall (Nolo)

The Wealthy Barber: Everyone's Common-Sense Guide to Becoming Financially Independent by David B. Chilton (Prima)

Software: *Quicken Financial Planner* (Intuit), *WEALTH-BUILDER* (Reality Technology)

Insurance

How to Get Your Money's Worth in Home and Auto Insurance by Barbara Taylor (McGraw Hill)

Smart Questions to Ask Your Insurance Agent: A Guide to Buying the Right Insurance for Your Family's Future by Dorothy Leeds (Harper)

Investing

Beating the Street by Peter Lynch (Simon & Schuster)

Bogle on Mutual Funds: New Perspectives for the Intelligent Investor by John C. Bogle (Irwin Professional)

Buying Stocks without a Broker by Charles Carlson (McGraw Hill)

Investor Beware! How to Protect Your Money from Wall Street's Dirty Tricks by John Lawrence Allen (Wiley)

The 100 Best Stocks to Own in America by Gene Walden (Dearborn)

Parenting

Kiplinger's Money Smart Kids (and Parents Too!) by Janet Bodnar (Kiplinger's)

Piggy Bank to Credit Card: Teach Your Child the Financial Facts of Life by Linda Barbanel (Crown)

Securing Your Child's Future: A Financial and Legal Planner for Parents by Winifed Conkling (Fawcett)

Real Estate

The Common-Sense Mortgage: How to Cut the Cost of Home Ownership by $100,000 or More by Peter G. Miller (Harper)

The HomeBuyer's Kit and The HomeSellers Kit by Edith Lank (Dearborn)

How to Buy a Home with No (or Little) Money Down by Martin Shenkman (Wiley)

How to Sell Your Home in 5 Days by William Effros (Workman)

Small Business

Dive Right in the Sharks Won't Bite: The Entrepreneurial Woman's Guide to Success by Jane Wesman (Dearborn)

How to Start, Run, and Stay in Business by Gregory F. Kishel (Wiley)

Making Money with Your Computer at Home by Paul and Sarah Edwards (Tarcher)

COMMON INVESTMENT TERMS

T his book has introduced you to the basic concepts of personal finance. In explaining these concepts, definitions and examples have been provided. What follows is a brief glossary of some of the more important terms used in the investment world.

Next time someone starts talking about some scheme that made quick profits, you can see whether the person knows what he or she is doing with the money. Or when you skim through ads in the financial section of the newspaper, you'll know whether you should pursue a particular investment or perhaps rethink your own portfolio.

401(k) plan   This is an increasingly popular retirement plan that lets you put aside pretax earnings; these funds are often matched by your employer.

annual percentage rate (APR)   This is the percent interest that you would pay during a year for money you borrow.

annuities   These are contracts with an insurance company that guarantee either a fixed or variable payment for some future time period.

assets   These are things that you own. Financial assets can be savings accounts, stocks, bonds, etc. Real assets include your home, jewelry, and collectibles.

bank liquid account   Another term for a savings or passbook account.

bear market   When prices on the stock market are falling, it is referred to as a bear market.

blue-chip   Common stock of well-known companies, such as IBM and GE, are known as blue-chip stocks.

bonds   These are loans that are made to private companies or government agencies. In return for lending the money, bondholders receive back interest over the term of the loan. The interest rate varies on the length of the loan and the type of bond.

bull market   When prices on the stock market are rising, it is referred to as a bull market.

capital gains   If you sell an investment at a higher price than what you paid for it, you have profits, known as capital gains. Usually, you will have to pay taxes on these gains.

certificates of deposit (CDs)   Available primarily from banks, you put a certain amount of money on deposit for a specific period of time. Your money earns interest, but there is a penalty for taking the money out of the CD before the maturity date.

common stock   You own shares in a public company. Common stockholders can vote on company matters and usually receive dividends.

debt   This refers to the amount of money or services you owe, such as for credit cards, car loans, mortgage, etc.

dividend Regular payments made by a company to its shareholders. You may choose to participate in a *dividend reinvestment plan,* in which your dividends are used to buy additional shares of stock.

Dow Jones Industrial Average A numerical average index of the performance of 30 stocks of well-known companies, known as blue-chip stocks. Other stocks are rated against this index to gauge their performance.

employee stock ownership plan (ESOP) A plan whereby a company issues stock to its employees, allowing them to become part owners of the company.

escrow This is money or property that is held in an account until terms of a contract are met by both parties. It is often used in mortgage transactions.

Federal Deposit Insurance Corporation (FDIC) This is the government agency that insures bank accounts.

futures market Commodities markets that trade in items such as coffee, gold, sugar, cotton, etc.

guaranteed investment contract (GIC) An option available in retirement plans that lets you select conservative investments that guarantee a certain rate of return.

index A statistical device that shows whether movement has been up or down from another period of time. Well-known indices include the consumer price index or the Standard & Poor's Index of Leading Economic Indicators.

individual retirement account (IRA) A tax-sheltered retirement vehicle.

initial public offering (IPO) This is the time a company first sells stock to the general public.

Keogh plan A retirement plan for self-employed people and those who own small businesses.

load Fees charged by mutual funds.

margin account A brokerage account that lets stockholders borrow against their account holdings to buy additional stock.

mutual funds A type of investment where funds of many investors are pooled together and invested, under the guidance of a professional fund manager.

odd lot This refers to buying less than 100 shares of stock at one time.

prospectus The legal document describing the company and offering, used when funds or companies are selling stock or fund shares.

real estate investment trust (REIT) A type of investment that puts money into real estate in order to earn profits for the investors.

return This is the amount of money you make on your investment.

risk This is the chance you take when investing that you may lose some or all of your principal.

rollover The act of moving your money from one investment, such as an IRA, into another investment. There are rules governing rollovers so that you don't pay taxes on the rollover funds.

Series EE savings bonds Bonds issued by the U.S. government that guarantee a certain rate of interest.

simplified employee pension (SEP) A type of retirement plan that both employees and employers contribute to.

treasury issues These include *bills, bonds,* and *notes.* They are issued by the federal government in different amounts from $1,000 and up and have different maturity periods.

zero-coupon bond Bonds that you buy for less than their face value for a set period of time. You receive no interest but are guaranteed to get the full face value at maturity.

INDEX

A

A. M. Best rating service for insurance, 96

Accidental death insurance policies, 113–14

Adjusted gross income (AGI) for tax returns, 135, 175

Aggressive growth funds, types of investments by, 52

Alimony payment obligations not affected by bankruptcy, 37

Alternative Qualification Program of Freddie Mac, 82–83

American Association of Individual Investors, 61

American Association of Retired Persons (AARP), medical insurance information from, 110

American Express card, 31

American Institute of Certified Public Accountants (AICPA), 138

Ameritas Life insurance company, 111

Annual fees for credit cards, 30–31

Annual percentage rate (APR) for credit cards, 30

Annuities
for college expenses, 130–131
deferred, 175
fixed, 176
as long-term investment, 64
penalties for early withdrawals from, 176
relative returns on, 64–65
for retirement income, 175–76
from trusts, 158
as untaxed until payments are received, 64
variable, 64, 176

Application fee for home equity loans, 40

Assets
 balance sheet listing of, 24–25
 to discuss in will, 149–50, 152
 insurance to protect your,
  93–114
 knowing your, 66
 ownership of, 159–60
 to pay off debts after your
  passing, 153
 trust funded with estate's, 156
Attorney to review contract
 on home purchase, 79
 on home sold at auction, 78
Attorney to write your will,
 149–50
Attorney's fees for buying a
 home, 73
Au pair child care provider, costs
 of, 120
Auction option for buying a
 home, 77–78
Auto loans, 38–39
Automobile insurance, 94,
 99–101
 bodily injury liability in,
  99–100
 choosing new car on basis of
  rate of, 101
 collision damage section of, 99
 comprehensive coverage in, 99
 discounts for, 100–101
 medical coverage in, 100
 "no fault" states and, 100
 property damage liability
  in, 100
 raising deductible to save
  money on, 101
 for teenagers, 101
 uninsured motorist coverage
  in, 100

B
Baby boomers, low savings rate
 of, 162
Back-end (redemption) fees for
 mutual funds, 55
Baird, Zoe, 119
Balance sheet of income and ex-
 penses, creating personal,
 24–26
Balanced funds, types of investments by, 52
Bank loan to establish credit
 history, 31
Bank statements, filing, 9
BankCard Holders of America
 for list of low interest rate
  credit cards, 30
 for list of no-fee and low-fee
  credit cards, 31
Bankruptcy, Chapter 7 and
 Chapter 13, 37
*Beardstown Ladies Common-
 sense Investment Guide, The,*
 62
Better Business Bureau, checking on mortgage broker, 82
Birth certificate, filing, 147
Blue-chip stocks as low and
 moderate risk invest-
 ments, 44
Bond funds
 for college savings, 127
 for retirement portfolio, 177
 types of investments by, 52
Bonds
 performance of, 57
 ratings of, 64
 relative returns on, 64
 volatility of, 63
 ways to buy, 63

as one of three sources of
money for retirement,
169–71
question of stability of, 162
for retirement income, 163, 170
of spouse's versus your earnings, 171
taxes on, 170
when to apply for, 177
Social Security card, filing,
147–48
Social Security taxes for child
care provider, 119
"Special needs" trust, 158–59
Spending
children's management of
their own, 22
computer programs for tracking, 23
publications about reducing, 22
reducing, 21–24
"Spendthrift" trust, 159
Sprinkling rights to trust custodian, 158–59
Stafford Loan Program for student loans, 129
Standard & Poor's Corporation
rating service for insu-
rance, 96
State and local income tax, 134
municipal and state bonds as
often free from, 64
U.S. savings bonds as free
from, 51
Stock
abbreviation for, 58
common, 57
exchanges listing, 57–58
growth and aggressive-growth,
college savings based
on, 126

long-term performance of, 57,
125–26, 173
preferred, 57
price of, 58
reasons for holding onto,
65–66
reasons why companies
sell, 57
reasons why fledgling in-
vestors should avoid buying,
51–52
research before you buy, 59, 60
volume of traded, 59
ways to buy, 60–63
ways to make money by in-
vesting in, 58
Stock exchanges, 57–58
Stock funds
for college savings, 126–27
determining percentage of investment to place in, 55–56
for 401(k) plan holdings,
173–74
performance during 1987
crash of, 53
splitting investment between
international fund and, 55
Stock market, understanding,
57–63
Stock tables in newspapers,
definitions of columns in,
58–59
Stockholders, preferred, 57

T
T-bill, minimum investment
for, 50
T-note
as conservative invest-
ment, 49
minimum investment for, 50

Also from Prima

Last Chance Financial Planning Guide
It's Not Too Late to Plan for Your Retirement If You Start Now

Anthony Spare
with Paul Ciotti

U.S. $15.00
Can. $19.95
ISBN: 0-7615-0836-8
paperback / 240 pages

"There is no sure way to make money. But there are lots of sure ways to lose money...the best of which is to be ignorant. Spare goes a long way in taking the ignorance out of investing."
—Arthur B. Laffer, V.A. Canto and Associates

This clear-eyed, upbeat book shows you how to ensure a worry-free retirement by investing in unloved, unappreciated, "cheap" stocks. You'll learn how to cope with the coming Social Security shortfall, plan your retirement, build your portfolio, and ferret out those humble but high-returning stocks that conventional wisdom overlooks.

To order, call 1-800-632-8676
Visit us online at www.primapub.com